Children's Devotions

Frances Ridley Havergal

Children's Devotions

*A month of devotions
for mornings and evenings*

Frances Ridley
Havergal

© This edition Copyright 2004 Christian Focus Publications
ISBN 1-85792-973-X

Published by Christian Focus Publications
Geanies House, Fearn, Tain, Ross-shire
IV20 1TW, Scotland, Great Britain
www.christianfocus.com
email:info@christianfocus.com
The version of the scripture used in this edition is an editorial
paraphrase of the authorised version.

Cover design Catherine Mackenzie
Printed, Nørhaven Paperback A/S, Denmark

This book was given
with love to

....

on

....

from

....

How this book was written

A little girl called Ethel was away from home on a week's visit. The first night, when she was tucked up in bed, and just ready for a goodnight kiss, I said, 'Now, shall I give you a little pillow?'

Ethel lifted her head to see what was under it, and said, 'I have got one, Auntie!'

'It was another sort of pillow that I meant to give you; I wonder if you will like it?'

Ethel realised that it was not a pillowcase to sleep on but she still did not understand, and so she laughed and said, 'Do tell me at once, Auntie, what you mean; don't keep me waiting to guess!'

Then I told her that, just as we want a soft pillow to lay our heads down upon at night, our hearts wanted a pillow too, something to rest upon, some true, sweet word that we might go to sleep upon happily and peacefully. And that it was a good plan always to take a little text for our pillow every night. So she had one that night, and the next night.

The third night I was prevented from coming up till long after Ethel should have been asleep. But there were the bright eyes peeping out robin-redbreast fashion, and a reproachful little voice said, 'Auntie, you have not given me any little pillow tonight!'

'Then, do you really care about having the little pillows given you, Ethel?'

'Oh, *of course* I do!' was the answer. She did not seem to think there could possibly be any doubt about it. Certainly the way in which she said that '*of course!*' showed that *she* had no doubt about it!

So it seemed that perhaps other little ones would like to have 'little pillows' put ready for every night. For even little hearts are sometimes very weary, and want something to rest upon; and a happy little heart, happy in the love of Jesus, will always be glad to have one of his own sweet words to go to sleep upon.

So here are thirty-one 'little pillows,' not to be used all at once, nor even two at a time, but one for every night in the month. The little texts are so short, that they will need no learning; but when you have read the explanation, you will be able to keep the text quite safely and easily in your mind.

Read the little book before you kneel down to say your evening prayers, because I hope what you read will always remind you of something to pray about. And then, when you lie down and shut your eyes, let your heart rest on the 'little pillow' till 'he gives his beloved sleep.'

But in the morning we want something to arouse us and to help us to go brightly and bravely through the day. So there are also some 'Morning Bells' to waken up little hearts and to remind them to walk with Jesus. May he who loves the little ones bless this tiny effort to help them to follow him day by day.

Contents

It is so good that these devotions
will be in print again.
I recommend them to parents.
They are warm and
spiritually direct,
and will encourage children
in their faith.
SHARON JAMES

Christ's Childhood

'Your holy child Jesus'
Acts 4:30

If I asked, 'How old are you?' you would give an exact answer. Perhaps you could tell me how many years old you are as well as how many months and days? Have you heard the story of Jesus as a little baby? Perhaps you have even have heard about Jesus when he was twelve years old in the temple? But have you ever thought of him as being exactly your own age? He was once really just as old as you are this very day! He knows

13

what it is to be five, seven, eight years old, ten and a half, or nine and three quarters – or whatever you may be. God's word has only told us one thing about Jesus during those years – that he was a holy child.

What is 'holy'? It is everything that is perfectly beautiful, good and loveable, without anything to spoil it. This is what Jesus was when he was your age. He was gentle, brave, considerate, unselfish, noble, truthful, obedient, loving, kind and forgiving – everything you can think of that you ever admired or loved in anyone else was all found in him – not only outside but inside, for he was 'holy.'

Why did he live all this time as a child on earth instead of staying in heaven till it was time to come and die for you? One reason was, so that he could leave you a beautiful example, so that you might wish to be like him and ask for the Holy Spirit to make you like him. But the other was even more gracious and wonderful; it was because of Jesus Christ 'we might become the righteousness of God.' That is, that all Christ's goodness and holiness may be given to you, because you do not have any of your own. God will then smile on you for Jesus' sake, just as if you had been perfectly obedient and truthful and unselfish and good. He will then give you Jesus' reward, which you never deserved at all, but which Jesus deserved for you. Jesus took your sins and gives you his righteousness; he took your punishment and gives you his reward. There is a swap, or exchange, if you will only accept it!

I'm glad my blessed Saviour
Was once a child like me,
To show how pure and holy
His little ones might be.
And if I try to follow
His footsteps here below,
He never will forget me.
Because he loves me so.

The Invitation

'Come to Me'
Matthew 11:28

Aren't these lovely words? Jesus is saying them to you.

How do I know this? Well, these words are written for every one that is weary and burdened. Do you know what it is to be weary and tired sometimes? Perhaps you know what it is to feel tired of trying to be good – weary with wishing you could be better. So, you see, it is to *you* that he says 'Come!'

And if you have not yet come to Jesus, you are burdened too, even if you do not feel it; because the burden of sin that you are carrying is heavy enough to sink you down into hell, unless Jesus takes it from you. So it is to *you* that he says 'Come!'

And just in case you should think he says it to grown-up people only, he said, 'Suffer the little children to come to me.' Are you a child? Then it is to you that he says 'Come!'

Do you say, 'If he were here, and if I could see him, I would like to come.' But remember that he *is* here, as really and truly as you are. Suppose your mother and you were in a dark room together, and she said, 'Come to me!' you would not stop to say, 'I would come if I could see you.' You would say, 'I am coming, mother!' and you would soon feel your way across the room, and be safe by her side. Not seeing her would not make any difference.

Jesus calls you now. He is in this room. Say to him, 'I am coming, Lord Jesus!' and ask him to stretch out his hand and help you. He will draw you close to himself.

Yes, to *himself,* the blessed, beloved Lord Jesus, who loved you and gave himself for you, who has waited so patiently for you, who calls you because he wants you to come and be his own little lamb, will hold you and bless you. Do not keep him waiting any longer – 'come.'

Will you not come to him for life?
Why will ye die, oh why?
He gave his life for you, for you!
The gift is free, the word is true!
Will ye not come?
Oh why will ye die?

Our Great Example

'Even Christ pleased not himself'
Romans 15:3

Do you really wish to follow the footsteps of the holy child Jesus? Have you asked God to make you more like him? Are you ready to begin today? Then here is a motto for today – 'Even Christ pleased not himself.' You should try to imitate him. You are sure to have plenty of opportunities to try this out. You will then be giving good things to others as well as to your dear Saviour and this will show them and him

19

that you mean what you say and mean what you pray.

Perhaps *'Even Christ pleased not himself'* seems a rather sad thing to read in the morning! But if you really wish to be like Christ, you will soon find that these words will help you over all sorts of difficulties, and save you from all sorts of sins and troubles.

When you cheerfully give something to someone else that you really wanted for yourself, and if you do this for Jesus' sake you will be very happy. You should try this. When you choose to do what your conscience tells you would please the Lord Jesus this will give you joy. When you choose to please the Lord Jesus instead of pleasing yourself this will make you happy. It is God's grace that helps us to do this. Ask God to help you please him instead of pleasing yourself.

If you have never tried it yet, begin today.

It will be like discovering a brand new happiness that you have not known before.

What would have happened to us if Christ had only 'pleased himself', and had stayed in his own glorious home instead of coming down to save us? Think of that when you are tempted to please yourself instead of pleasing him. And when you remember that Jesus pleased not himself because he loved you perhaps this will help you to try and please him and to please others for his sake.

> If washed in Jesus' blood,
> Then bear his likeness too!
> And as you onward press,
> Ask, 'What would Jesus do?'

> Give with a full, free hand;
> God freely gives to you!
> And check each selfish thought
> With, 'What would Jesus do?'

Accepted

'Accepted in the Beloved'
Ephesians 1:6

WHO is 'accepted in the Beloved'? *You*, if you have come to your heavenly Father, asking him to receive you for Jesus Christ's sake. Do you want to know that you are saved and forgiven? Then take all the beautiful comfort and joy of these words! They are for you just as much as for any grown-up person.

Ask him *now* to give you faith to believe these words for yourself. At the same time you will try to understand what these words really mean for you.

Suppose a king said to some poor children that he would take a child, *any* child to stay with him in his beautiful palace. But the child must really wish to go and must ask him to take them. Imagine you were a poor child with no home to go to and no one to love – suppose you wished the king would take you. Then the king beckons you, and the prince himself leads you to his father, and tells you to say what you want, and you say, 'I want to go, please take me!' Will the king break his word and *not* take you? No, because he *never* breaks his promise and he beckoned you himself. That was what made you go. The prince, his beloved son, took your hand and brought you. Would the king send away any child who his son brought? There can be no mistake; he won't reject you, so you *must* be 'accepted.'

God the Father is our heavenly King, and Jesus Christ his one and only Son. It is true that every one who has come to Jesus, even if only a little girl or boy, is 'accepted in the Beloved.' Accepted, because God has said, 'I will receive you.' Accepted, because he has called and drawn you or you never would have wanted to come. Accepted, because the Beloved One has made it possible for you to come to God because he has shed his own blood, and he saves *all* that come to God by him. Accepted, not because you are worth God's accepting, but 'accepted in the Beloved.' You are accepted because of Jesus Christ.

Safe in the arms of Jesus, Safe on his gentle breast,
There, by his love o'ershadowed,
Sweetly my soul shall rest.
Hark! 'tis the voice of angels,
Borne in a song to me,
Over the fields of glory, Over the jasper sea.

Upholding

'Hold me up and I shall be safe.'
Psalm 119:117

The path is not easy. There are rough stones over which we may stumble, if we are not walking very carefully. There are places which look smooth, but they are more dangerous than the rough ones, for they are slippery. There are little holes hidden under flowers, which may catch our feet and give us a bad fall. There are muddy ditches, into which we may slip and get wet and dirty.

25

How are we to walk safely along such a path? We want a strong, kind hand to hold us up and to hold us always; a hand that will hold ours tightly and lovingly. Our lives are like this path - we can fall into sin, we can have difficulties. But it is like what one old woman said, 'Not my grip of Christ, but Christ's grip of me!' Yes, Christ's loving hand is 'able to keep you from falling'; let your hand rest in the hand of Jesus, and then you will be able to walk safely and your foot shall not stumble. The Lord will keep you from sinning. God will help you and protect you.

But do not be half hearted this morning! Do not say to God, 'Hold me up,' and then complain, 'but I am sure I shall stumble and fall!' Remember to say these words instead, 'Hold me up and I shall be safe!' If you trust God to do just what you ask and let him hold you up - you will be safe.

It would be hard to find a prayer in the Bible

without a promise to match it, so David says, 'Uphold me, according to your Word.'

What has he said about it? More than there is room for on this page.

'I the Lord your God will hold your right hand.'

'Yes, I will uphold you.'

'He will not allow your foot to be moved.'

'When you run you shall not stumble.'

'Yes, he shall be held up.'

'He shall keep your foot from being taken.'

'He will keep the feet of his saints.'

Seven promises in answer to your one little prayer!

> 'I the Lord am with thee,
> Be thou not afraid!
> I will help and strengthen,
> Be thou not dismayed!
> Yea, I will uphold thee
> With my own right hand;
> Thou art called and chosen
> In my sight to stand.'

The Red Hand

'I, even I, am he that blots out your transgressions'
Isaiah 43:25

There was once a boy who was deaf and couldn't speak and his name was John. Though he never heard any other voice, he heard the voice of Jesus, knew it, loved it, and followed it.

John could speak partly with his fingers and partly with signs and one day he told the lady who had taught him his signs that he had had a wonderful dream. God had shown him a great black book; and all John's sins were written in it, so many, so black!

God had shown him hell, all open and fiery, waiting for him, because of all these sins. But Jesus Christ had come and put his *red hand*, red with the blood of his cross, all over the page, and the red hand, the *dear* red hand, had blotted all John's sins out; and when God held up the book to the light, he could not see one left!

Now his sweet word to you tonight is, 'I, even I, am he that blots out your transgressions.' Will you believe it? 'Only believe,' and 'according to your faith it shall be to you.' It is not a made-up story or just a feeling, but this is God's truth, that Jesus Christ's blood has been shed – nothing can alter that; and his precious blood blots out our sins; as Paul says (Colossians. 2: 14), 'Blotting out the handwriting of ordinances that was against us.'

And oh how much there is to blot out! – sins

29

that you have forgotten, and sins that you did not think were sins at all, besides those you know of – today, yesterday, all the past days of your life. And all these written in his book!

Do you want to have them blotted out for ever? Do you pray, 'Blot out my iniquities?' do you want to know that they are blotted out? Then just believe that it is true, and true for you – 'I *have* blotted out as a thick cloud your sins: return to me, for I have redeemed you.'

I am trusting thee, Lord Jesus,
Trusting only thee;
Trusting thee for full salvation,
Great and free.

I am trusting thee for cleansing
Through the crimson flood;
Trusting thee to make me holy
By thy blood.

What can I do?

'Bear one another's burdens and so
fulfil the law of Christ.' Galatians 6:2

This verse is talking to us about burdens. Perhaps you never thought that anyone around you had any? Then if you want to keep this law of Christ, the first thing you need to do is to find out who has a burden and how you can help. You will not have to wait long. There are very few people who do not have a burden. You may think that you won't be able to help someone who has to carry a great burden, but

31

sometimes people who have great burdens have little burdens too. It can be a great help when someone comes along to help that person with one or two of these.

If your mother was carrying a heavy parcel, would it not help her if you took two or three little ones out of her hand and carried them for her? Perhaps she has troubles that you do not even know about and you see she looks tired and anxious. Perhaps she is even more tired because your little brother or sister wants to be looked after or amused.

Now if you put away your game or stopped reading your book and began to play quietly with your little brother or sister that would be a great help. This would be helping your mother with one of her burdens. Never mind if it is a little burden. You may think that it is actually a very easy burden to carry. It is still worth it, because it is keeping the law of Christ!

If for a moment a burden that you have taken up does seem rather hard – think of what the Lord Jesus has done for you! Think how he took up the heaviest burdens of all for you, when he carried our sins in his own body on the cross! He did not drop that burden, but carried it till he died under it. Think of that and it will be easy then to carry something for his sake.

Now be on the watch all today for burdens to carry for others. See how many you can find out and pick up and carry away! Depend upon it, you will not only make it a brighter day for others, but for yourself too!

> *Little deeds of kindness,*
> *Little words of love,*
> *Make our earth an Eden,*
> *Like the heaven above.*

God's Love

'I have loved you, saith the Lord'
Malachi 1:2

These words are like a nice soft pillow for you to rest on. When you read these words tonight they should help you go to sleep they are so comforting. But a pillow is of no use if you only look at it. You must lay your head down upon it, and then you rest. So, do not only think, 'Yes, these are nice words'; but believe it, and lay your heart down restfully upon it; and say, 'Yes, the Lord Jesus loves me!'

How different these words are from what we should have expected! We should have expected God to say, 'I will love you, if you will love me.' But no! He says, 'I *have* loved you.' Yes, he has loved you already! He loves you now, and will love you always.

But you say, 'I wish I knew whether he loves *me*!' But Jesus *tells* you so. He can't say any more! Here are his words – 'I have loved you, says the Lord.' It is TRUE, and all you have to do is believe it, and be glad, and tell Jesus how glad you are that he loves you.

But you say, 'Yes, I know he loves good people; but I am so naughty!' Then he has a special word for you: 'God commends his love toward us, in that, while we were yet sinners, Christ died for us.' He says nothing about 'good people,' but tells you that he loved you so much, while you were naughty, that he sent the Lord Jesus, his own dear, dear Son, to die for you. Could he do more than that?

He says in the same verse (Malachi 1:2), '*But you ask, "How have you loved us?"*' He loves us here and now and he loved us then. It is important to love God, but it is more important that he loves you, and sent his Son to suffer instead of you. When you lie down to go to sleep, think how many answers you can find to that question, 'How have you loved us?' There are many ways that God shows us that he loves us. Go to sleep thinking on these soft, safe words: 'I have loved you, says the Lord!'

> *I am so glad that our Father in heaven*
> *Tells of his love in the book he has given,*
> *Wonderful things in the Bible I see:*
> *This is the dearest, that Jesus loves me.*

> *Oh, if there's only one song I can sing*
> *When in his beauty I see the great King;*
> *This shall my song in eternity be,*
> *Oh, what a wonder, that Jesus loves me!*

Instruments

'Yield… your members as instruments of righteousness to God.' Romans 6:13

Sometimes bells can sound tuneful and pleasant – sometimes they are loud and clanging. Perhaps these words this morning don't sound quite so pleasant as some of the other words we have read. But listen for a few minutes and you will hear the music.

What are your members? Hands, feet, lips, eyes, ears and so on. What are you to do with them? 'Yield' them, that is, give them up

37

altogether, hand them over to God. What for? That he may use them as instruments of righteousness. That is, just as we should take an instrument of music like a flute or a piano and make music with it, so God wants to take your hands and feet and all the parts of your body and use them to do right and good things with.

If you give yourself to God, every part of you is to be God's servant, an instrument for him to use.

Your hands will no longer serve Satan by striking or pinching; your feet will not kick or stamp, nor drag and dawdle, when they should run briskly on an errand; your lips will not pout; your tongue will not move to say a naughty thing. Every bit of your body will stop serving Satan and find something to do for God; for if you 'yield' them to God, he will really take them and use them.

He will tell your hands to pick up what your tired mother has dropped. Your fingers will help to make something for a poor child or an old person. God will tell your feet to run on errands of kindness and help. He will help your lips to sing happy hymns, which will cheer and comfort somebody, even if you never know of it. He will use your eyes for reading to someone who cannot read for themselves such as a blind person or a little child. You will be quite surprised to find how many ways God will really use even your body, if you give your whole self to him. It will be so nice! You will never be miserable again with 'nothing to do!'

> *Take my hands and let them move*
> *At the impulse of thy love.*
> *Take my feet and let them be*
> *Swift and 'beautiful' for thee.*

God's Care

'He that keeps you will not slumber'
Psalm 121:3

Sometimes little children wake in the night, and feel lonely, and a little bit afraid. This is not because of the darkness; for if others are with them, talking and moving about, they do not mind it at all. But it is the stillness, the strange silence when everybody is fast asleep.

Everybody? No! The One who loves you best of all is watching you all the time; the One who cares for you never sleeps – 'He that keeps you will not slumber.' He is there all the time, never leaving you one moment alone, never going away at all. It makes no difference to him that it is very dark, for 'the darkness and the light are both the same' to him. And all through the dark hours he 'keeps you'; keeps you from everything that could hurt or even frighten you, so that you may safely and quietly take the sweet sleep he gives you.

He 'keeps you'; only think who is your keeper! The mighty God, who can do everything, and can see everything. When God looks after you you do not need to be afraid. It is very nice to know that 'he shall give his angels charge over you to keep you'; but it is even better still to think that God himself keeps us. As if he wanted us to be very sure of it, and to leave us no excuse for ever being afraid any more, he even says it three times over, 'he that keeps you will not slumber.' 'Behold, he that keeps Israel shall neither slumber nor sleep.' 'The Lord is your keeper.' What more could he say?

Now what will you say to him if you wake in the night and feel lonely in the stillness? Remember these wonderful words that he has given to you: *'He that keeps you will not slumber'* these words are like a pillow that he has given you at night to rest upon. Say to God 'I will trust, and not be afraid.'

He will take care of you!
All through the night
Jesus, the Shepherd,
His little one keeps:
Darkness to him is the same as the light;
He never slumbers and he never sleeps.

Willing and Glad

'Then the people rejoiced, for that they offered willingly.' 1 Chronicles 29:9

We thought yesterday morning about giving our body to God for him to use. Did you think you would like to do this? Did you yield? If you did, you will understand this morning's text! David the king asked his people to help in bringing offerings for God's house and service and God made them all willing to bring what they could. And what then? *'Then* the people rejoiced ... because with perfect heart they offered willingly to the Lord. And did eat and drink on that day before the Lord with great gladness.'

See what came of offering willingly to the Lord – they 'rejoiced,' and everything they did, even eating and drinking, was 'with great gladness.' When someone offers themselves willingly to the Lord they will be very happy - in fact they cannot be more happy than when they do this. The Lord gives them much, much, more in return. He gives them peace and gladness and blessing, beyond what they ever expected to have.

But it was not only the people who had such a glad day, but 'David the king also rejoiced with great joy.' Those who loved their king and remembered how much sorrow he had gone through and how many battles he had fought for them, must have been glad indeed to see him rejoicing because they had offered willingly. And I think our King, *your* King Jesus, rejoices

over us when he has made us able (verse 14)
to offer ourselves willingly to him. The best
thing is that Jesus, who suffered for us and
who fought the great battle of our salvation
for us, our own beloved King, 'will rejoice over
you with joy; he will quiet you with his love; he
will rejoice over you with singing.'

In full and glad surrender,
I give myself to thee,
Thine utterly and only
and evermore to be!
O Son of God, who lovest me,
I will be thine alone,
And all I have and all I am,
shall henceforth be thine own.

What Christ bore for us

'The Lord has laid on him the iniquity of us all'
Isaiah 53:6

Where are your sins? Wherever they are, God's terrible punishment must fall. Even if there was only one sin, and that one sin was hidden away down in your heart, God's wrath would find it out, and punish it. It could not escape.

But you know of many more than one; and God knows of more still. And so the great question for you is, where are they? If he finds them on you, his wrath and anger must fall on you. But if they are put *somewhere else*, you are safe, for he loves you, and only hates your sins. Where can that wonderful 'somewhere else' be? Tonight's text tells you that God laid them on Jesus. Why did his terrible wrath fall on his beloved, holy Son? Because he had laid our sins on Jesus, and Jesus took them, and was willing to bear them or carry them, so that all the dreadful punishment might fall on him instead of us. Instead of *you*!

When the great drops of blood fell down to the ground from Jesus' beloved head in the Garden of Gethsemane, it was because the Lord had laid on him *your* iniquity, *your* sin. When he hung by his pierced hands and feet upon the cross, alone in the great darkness of God's wrath and anger, it was because he was bearing *your* punishment, because *your* sins were laid upon him, so that they might not be found upon you, and punished upon you.

Satan will try to persuade you not to believe that *your* sins were laid upon Jesus. He will try to make sure that you are always doubting it; but God says that your sins were laid upon Christ! Which will you believe? God or Satan?

Again look at the solemn question, 'Where are your sins?' and then look at Jesus, suffering and dying for you, and answer boldly, 'On Jesus! For 'the Lord has laid on him the iniquity of us all.'

And so he died! And this is why
He came to be a man and die:
The Bible says he came from heaven,
That we might have our sins forgiven.

He knew how wicked men had been,
He knew that God must punish sin;
So, out of pity, Jesus said,
He'd bear the punishment instead.

Faithfulness

'Faithful over a few things'
Matthew 25:21,23

The servant who had only two talents to trade with, but traded faithfully with them, had just the same glorious words spoken to him as the servant who had five talents: 'Well done, good and faithful servant: you have been faithful over a few things... enter into the joy of your Lord.' Wouldn't it be wonderful to listen to the gracious voice of Jesus saying those wonderfully gracious words to *you*!

But could he say them to you? Are you 'faithful over the few things?' He has given everyone, even the youngest, a few things to be faithful over and so he has to you. Your 'few things' may be very few and very small things, but he expects you to be faithful over them.

What is 'being faithful over them?' It means doing the very best you can with them; doing as much for Jesus as you can with your money, even if you have very little; doing as much for him as you can with your time; doing whatever duties he gives you as well as you can, – your lessons, your work, the little things that you are asked to do every day, the little things that you have promised or started to do for others. It means doing all these even if someone sees you or not and even if someone knows about it or not.

Perhaps you have just given a big sigh over all this because you know that there are many things in which you have not been faithful; you know you do not deserve for Jesus to call you a 'good and faithful servant.' But come at once to your gracious Lord and ask him to forgive all the unfaithfulness and to make you faithful today. And then, even if it is only when you are doing a little work at school or at home you will remember these words to be, 'Faithful over a few things!'

Only, O Lord, in thy dear love,
Fit us for perfect rest above;
And help us, this and every day,
To live more near thee as we pray.

Peace through Blood

'Peace through the blood of his cross'
Colossians 1:20

If you are disobedient to your parents, you feel that there is something between them and you, like a little wall built up between you. Even though you know they love you and keep doing kind things for you as usual, you are not happy with them and keep away from them, and it is a sad day both for them and for you. For there is no *peace* between them and you, or in your own heart.

The Lord Jesus knew that it was just like this

with us, that there was something between us and God instead of peace, and this something was sin. And there never could be or can be any peace with God while there is sin, so, of course, there never could be any real peace in our hearts. We could never take away this wall of sin. If left to ourselves, we only keep building it higher and higher by fresh sins every day. And God has said, that 'without the shedding of blood there is no remission,' that is, no forgiveness, no taking away of sins. Now what has Jesus Christ done for us? He has made peace through his blood shed on the cross. He is the Lamb of God that takes away the sin of the world; and the sin was what stopped peace.

Think about his precious blood that was shed to take away your sins! Do you believe it? Then there is nothing between you and God, for that bleeding hand has broken down the wall; the blood has made peace, and you may come to your heavenly Father and receive his loving forgiveness, and know that you have peace with God, through Jesus Christ our Lord.

Precious blood that hath redeemed us,
All the price is paid!
Perfect pardon now is offered,
Peace is made.

Precious blood, whose full atonement
Makes us nigh to God!
Precious blood, our song of glory,
Praise and laud!

Precious, precious blood of Jesus,
Ever flowing free!
Oh believe it, oh receive it,
'Tis for thee!'

On My Account

'Put that on my account.'
Philemon verse 18

When Paul asked Philemon, in a most beautiful letter, to take back Onesimus, who had run away from him, he said, 'If he has wronged you, or owes you anything, put that on my account.' Onesimus had been a bad servant to Philemon; though he was now willing to come back and do better. But the problem was that he could not pay for the wrong things that he had done before. But Paul offered to pay all, so that Onesimus could return, 'not now as a servant,' but as a 'brother beloved.'

This is a lovely picture of what the Lord Jesus Christ does. He intercedes for us with God against whom we have sinned, and even though he knows how much we have sinned and owe God, he says, 'Put that on my account.'

And God has put it all on his account and the account has been paid, paid in blood. When 'the Lord laid on him the iniquity of us all,' Jesus saw and knew all your sins; and he said, 'Put that on my account.'

Oh what wonderful 'kindness and love of God our Saviour'! It should be like a silver bell, ringing softly and clearly whenever you are going to do something that is not right.

'Put *that* on my account!' Yes, that sin that you were on the very edge of committing! That angry word and that angry feeling that made you want to say it; that untrue word and the cowardliness which made you afraid to speak the exact truth; that proud look and the naughty pride of heart that made it come into your eyes: Jesus stands by and says patiently and lovingly, 'Put *that* on my account!'

Does it not make you wish, ten times more than ever, to be kept from sinning against such a Saviour?

> *Jesus, tender Saviour.*
> *Hast thou died for me?*
> *Make me very thankful*
> *In my heart to thee;*
> *When the sad, sad story*
> *Of thy grief I read,*
> *Make me very sorry*
> *For my sins indeed.*

Whiter than Snow

'Whiter than snow'
Psalm 51:7

This verse is about being 'Whiter than snow', but surely snow is whiter than anything else? Especially if you see it glittering in the sunshine on the top of a high mountain, where no dust can ever reach it. But some people have seen something that is as white as snow. The angel at the resurrection was as 'white as snow'; and Jesus on the Mount of Transfiguration was 'very white like snow.'

But what can be made 'whiter than snow?'

Well in this verse someone is asking 'Wash *me*, and *I* shall be whiter than snow!' So what is it that can be whiter than snow then? Why you of course. What, *me*? My naughty, sinful self? My soul so stained with sin, that I cannot make it or keep it clean at all? Yes, '*I* shall be whiter than snow,' if God washes me.

But water will not do this, and tears will not do it. Only one thing can do it thoroughly. 'The blood of Jesus Christ, God's Son, cleanses us from all sin.'

This is 'the fountain opened for sin and for uncleanness'; and ever since the precious blood was shed, it has always been open. It is open now, this very evening, ready for you to be washed in it, and made 'whiter than snow.'

Do not just think about it, but go to your heavenly Father, and ask him to wash you in the precious blood of Christ.

Be *willing* to be *really* washed. Do not be like some little children, who do not wish to have clean clothes put on, because they know they cannot go and play in the dirt. Be willing not to go back to the dirt any more.

And then *let* him wash you; do not just say the words, and think no more of it. Look at the precious blood of Jesus then ask him to show you how it was shed for you, and how it really cleanses from all sin. And then you will be ready to fall down at Jesus' feet, 'giving him thanks' for having washed even you.

> *Precious, precious blood of Jesus,*
> *Let it make thee whole!*
> *Let it flow in mighty cleansing*
> *O'er thy soul.*
>
> *Though thy sins are red like crimson,*
> *deep in scarlet glow,*
> *Jesu's precious blood can make them*
> *White as snow.*

White Garments

'Let your garments be always white.'
Ecclesiastes 9:8

But how do you keep clean and sin free? So often you are dirty again almost as soon as you have been washed clean! Yet God says, 'Always be clothed in white'; and he would not tell you to do what was impossible. Then how are you to keep your clothes white - or how are you to stop sinning? There is only one way to do this. Last night you found out how Jesus washes us 'whiter than snow' in his own precious blood, that

61

cleanses from all sin. But will he only cleanse you just for the moment? Is that all he is able and willing to do for you?

No, if you will trust in that precious blood and not turn away from it, he says that it cleanses and it *goes on cleansing*. You could not keep white and pure for five minutes; careless thoughts would come like dust and wrong words would be like great dark stains and before long some naughty deed would be like a sad fall in the mud and you would feel ashamed before the kind Saviour who still stands ready to cleanse you again. But Jesus never, never gives up. His precious blood '*goes on cleansing*,' so that our garments may be always white. But why then do we still sin? Perhaps you never thought of this. Ask Jesus this morning not only to wash you in the fountain of his precious blood, but *to keep you in it,* to *go on cleansing* you all day long. *Trust* him to do this and see if it is not the happiest day you ever spent!

And he can do all this for me,
Because in sorrow, on the tree,
He once for sinners hung;
And, having washed their sin away,
He now rejoices day by day,
To cleanse his little one.

Asking

'Ask for whatever you want me to give you,'
2 Chronicles 1:7

There had been a grand day in Israel. The young King Solomon had spoken to all the people, and to all the great men and captains and governors, and they had followed him to the tabernacle of the Lord, and he had gone up to the altar which Bezaleel had made nearly 500 years before, and had offered a thousand burnt-offerings. 'In that night,' when it was all over, and Solomon was quiet and alone, God appeared to Solomon, and said to him,

'Ask for whatever you want me to give you.' And Solomon took God at his word, and asked at once for what he felt he wanted most. And God kept his word, and gave him at once what he asked, and promised him a great deal more besides.

This is the message to you tonight, 'Ask for whatever you want me to give you.'

Think what you most want, and ask for that, for Jesus Christ's sake. You need not, like Solomon, ask for only one thing; you may want many things, and you may ask for them all. And God will give – he always does give to the real askers – more than you ask, more than you ever thought of asking.

Perhaps you say, 'I don't know what to ask.' Then begin by asking him to show you by his Holy Spirit what you really want, and to teach you to ask for it.

Then you say, 'Will he give me whatever I ask?'

Well, if you ask something which is not good for you, he loves you too much to give you that! But he will give you something better. But if you ask for something he has promised to give, you may be quite certain he will give it you. Remind your heavenly Father of his promises, as Solomon did (verse. 9). And you may ask and expect the answer at once, like Solomon, who said, 'Now, O Lord God!' and 'Give me now!'

Then listen to God's message, and now, this very evening, ask him for some of his promised gifts. And when you lie down, try to think of the different things which he has promised, and which you want, and turn every thought into the prayer, 'Give me now – for Jesus Christ's sake.'

Thou art coming to a King,
Large petitions with thee bring;
For his grace and power are such,
None can ever ask too much.

Made Beautiful

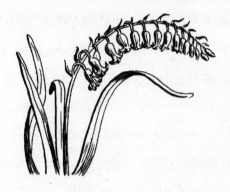

*'Let the beauty of the Lord our God
be upon us.' Psalm 90:17*

'How great is his beauty!' said Zechariah. How
can God's beauty be upon us? In two ways; try
to understand them and then ask that in both
ways the beauty of the Lord our God may be
upon you.

One way that God's beauty can be upon is
when he covers you with the robe of Jesus
Christ's righteousness, looking upon you not
as you are in yourself, all sinful and unholy, but

67

as if all the Saviour's beauty and holiness were yours, giving it to you for his sake. In this way he can call us 'perfect through my comeliness which I put upon you.' The other way is by giving you the beauty of holiness, for that is his own beauty; and though we never can be quite like him till we see him as he is, he can begin to make us like him even now. Look at a poor little colourless drop of water, hanging weakly on a blade of grass. It is not beautiful at all; why should you stop to look at it? Stay till the sun has risen and now look. It is sparkling like a diamond; and if you look at it from another side, it will be glowing like a ruby and then gleaming like an emerald. The poor little drop has become one of the brightest and loveliest things you ever saw. But is it its own brightness and beauty? No, if it slipped down to the ground out of the sunshine, it would be only a poor little dirty drop of water. So, if the

Sun of Righteousness, the glorious and lovely
Saviour, Christ Jesus, shines upon you, a little
ray of his own brightness and beauty will be
seen upon you. Sometimes we can see by the
happy light on a face that the Sun of
Righteousness, our Lord Jesus, is shining there;
but if he is really shining, there are sure to be
some of the beautiful rays of holiness, love,
joy, peace, gentleness, goodness, faith,
meekness, making the life even of a little child
very lovely.

> *Jesus, Lord I come to thee.*
> *Thou hast said I may;*
> *Tell me what my life should be,*
> *Take my sins away.*

> *Jesus, Lord, I learn of thee,*
> *In thy Word divine;*
> *Every promise there I see,*
> *May I call it mine!*

God's Benefits

'Forget not all his benefits'
Psalm 103:2

If a kind friend gave you a present of twenty pounds to buy all sorts of things with, would you not feel rather hurt if he kept saying to you, 'Do not forget that I gave you this'? Of course you would not forget, you would not be ungrateful. But what if you *did* forget, and used all your nice things and never remembered him at all, would it not make you feel ashamed if he came again and said very gently, 'Do not forget'?

Who do you think I am talking about? I don't really need to tell you, do I! You know! Have you forgotten all the good things that Jesus has given you? Have you forgotten to thank him for them? These blessings didn't just come all by themselves, did they? Please ask him now to forgive you for this sin of forgetfulness, for Jesus Christ's sake! And now that he has reminded you and forgiven you, ask him for the Holy Spirit to help you to remember his benefits instead of forgetting them.

'His benefits' means all the good things he has done for you, and all the good things he has given you. Try to count up 'his benefits' from just one day; and then think of the benefits he gave you yesterday, and last week, and all the year, and all your life since you were a baby! You will soon find that there are more than you can count, and you will begin to see how very much you have to thank him for. And then think about the great gift of Jesus Christ himself to be your Saviour and Redeemer, and the great gift of salvation through him, and all his promises of grace and glory!

David speaks of 'the multitude of his tender mercies,' and Isaiah tells of 'the multitude of his loving-kindnesses.' These are true and beautiful words. Will you not turn them into a song of thanksgiving? 'Bless the Lord, O my soul, and forget not all his benefits: Who crowns you with loving-kindness and tender mercies!'

> *Now my evening praise I give;*
> *Thou didst die that I might live;*
> *All my blessings come from thee,*
> *Oh how good thou art to me!*
>
> *Thou, my best and kindest friend,*
> *Thou wilt love me to the end;*
> *Let me love thee more and more,*
> *Always better than before.*

Pleasant Gifts

'Who gives us richly all things to enjoy.'
1 Timothy 6:17

Think a little this morning of God's great kindness to you. How *very* good he is to you! I know someone who says many times a day, *'Good* Lord Jesus!' or *'Kind* Lord Jesus!' She can't help saying it, just because he *is* so good and kind. It just seems so natural for her to look up again and again and say, *'Dear* Lord Jesus!' How *can* anybody go all day long and never see how good he is and never look up and bless him?

73

Particularly when it is a bright pleasant day, with lots more things than usual to enjoy! He 'gives.' Every single pleasant thing, every single bit of enjoyment comes to us from the Lord. We cannot get it, we do not earn it, we do not deserve it; but he *gives* lovingly and kindly and freely. Suppose he stopped giving, what would become of us?

God also gives to us 'Richly.' So richly, that if you tried to write down half his gifts to you, your hand would be tired long before you were done. You might easily make a list of the presents given to you on your birthday, but you could not make a list of what God gives you every day of your life.

'All things.' All the things you really need and many more besides. All that will do you good, many more than you would ever have thought of. All the things that he can fill your hands with and trust you to carry without stumbling and falling. *All* things, everything you have!

'To enjoy.' Now how kind this is! Not only 'to do us good,' but 'to enjoy.' So you see he wants you to be happy with what he gives you, to smile and laugh and be glad, not to be dismal and melancholy. If you do not enjoy what he 'gives,' that is your own fault, for he meant you to enjoy it. Look up to him with a bright smile and thank him for having given you richly all things to enjoy!

My joys to thee I bring,
The joys thy love hath given,
That each may be a wing
To lift me nearer heaven.
I bring them, Saviour, all to thee
For thou has purchased all for me.

Willing and Doing

*'It is God which works in you, both to will and
to do of his good pleasure'* Philippians 2.13.

These words may seem quite hard but it is these
hard words that will make many hard things quite
easy for you. Do you find it hard to be good?
I'm sure that you do find it hard to keep from
saying something naughty. It can be very hard to
keep down the angry feeling, even if you did
not say the angry word. It is certainly hard to do
a right thing when you do not like doing it and
quite impossible to make yourself wish to do it!

I am sure that you have sometimes asked God to help you to do the right thing and that he did help you; but did you ever think of asking him to make you *like* to do it?

Now, this is just what is meant by God's 'working in you to *will*.' It means that he can and will undertake the very thing which you cannot manage. He can and will 'take your will, and work it for you'; making you want to do what he wants you to do; making you like what he likes, and hate what he hates.

It is always easy to do what we like doing; so, when we have given up our will to him, and asked him to work it for us, it makes everything easy. It is then that we shall *want* to 'do according to his good pleasure,' and we shall be very happy in it. Trying to please God will not be fighting against our own wills, when God has taken our wills and is working them for us.

Do you not see what happy days there will be

if you just take God at his word about this? Try it and you will see! Tell him that you have found you cannot manage your will yourself, and that now you will give it up to him, and trust him, *from now*, not only to work in you to *do*, but to work in you to *will* also, 'according to his good pleasure.' God will help you trust and obey and he will make you want to trust and obey too.

> *Take my will, and make it thine;*
> *It shall be no longer mine.*

> *Take my heart, it is thine own;*
> *It shall be thy royal throne.*

Much More Than This

*'The Lord is able to give you much more
than this.' 2 Chronicles 25:8*

Amaziah, king of Judah, was going to war against
the Edomites. He thought he would make sure
of victory by hiring a hundred thousand soldiers
from the King of Israel and he paid them
beforehand a hundred talents, which was a lot of
money. But a man of God warned him not to let
the army of Israel go with him, for Israel had
forsaken the Lord and so he was not with them.
It seemed a great pity to waste all that money and

79

so Amaziah said, 'But what shall we do for the hundred talents which I have given to the army of Israel?' And the man of God answered, 'The Lord is able to give you much more than this.' So Amaziah simply obeyed and sent the soldiers away and trusted God to help him to do without them. Was it any wonder that he gained a great victory over the Edomites.

This teaches us that we should simply do the right thing and trust God at any costs. When you do this, you will find that, in hundreds of ways which you never thought of, 'the Lord is able to give you much more.' The trial comes in many different ways. Perhaps there is someone who is tempted to hurry over prayer and the Bible, because there is something else that they want done before breakfast. Perhaps someone might shut their purse when a call comes to give something for God's work, because they are afraid they will not have enough left at the end of the week. Another is tempted to cheat in a test in order to get the marks they are aiming for. Another is tempted not to tell the exact truth, or to conceal something. You must resist the Devil and do what you know is right and trust God for all the rest! For 'the Lord is able to give you much more than this,' whatever your *this* may be. And his smile and his blessing will always be 'more than this,' more than anything else!

> *Be brave to do the right,*
> *And scorn to be untrue,*
> *When fear would whisper 'yield'!*
> *Ask, 'What would Jesus do'?*

You know Lord

'O Lord, you know.'
Jeremiah 15:15

This text has been a comfort to many children and adults. Children are not always happy and they do not always get as much sympathy as they want, because their troubles are not exactly the same as grown-ups. Have you had troubles today? Have you felt sad and downhearted? Perhaps you haven't been able to explain why you feel troubled, so no one can comfort you because they just don't understand? Take this verse from Jeremiah as a little pillow to rest your tired heart on tonight. 'You know! You, Lord Jesus, kind Shepherd of the weary or wandering little lambs, you know all about it! You have heard the words that made me feel so sad; you saw what happened that troubled me; you know what I can not explain, you understand my thoughts; you were looking down into my heart all the time, and nothing is hidden from you! You know *all* the truth about it! And you know all that I cannot put into words at all!'

Do you feel comforted already when you know that he knows? It's enough to know that, isn't it? You know that he can do everything; so, surely, he can make things come right for you (really right, not perhaps what you imagine would be nicest and most right). And you know that he cares (that is, goes on caring) for you; so if he knows about your trouble, he cares about it too. And he not only cares, but loves. He would not have let this trouble touch his dear child unless he wanted it to be a little messenger. He is calling you to him to be comforted. He wants to show you that he is your best Friend, and to teach you the sweetness of saying, 'You know Jesus, you know!'

Jesus is our Shepherd
Wiping every tear;
Folded in his bosom,
What have we to fear?

'Only let us follow
Whither he doth lead;
To the thirsty desert,
Or the dewy mead.

The Doings of the King

'Whatsoever the king did pleased all the people.'
2 Samuel 3:36

David showed his love for someone who had been his enemy for a long time. But after all that David agreed to become Abner's friend and then when Abner died he showed all the people his tenderheartedness by weeping with them at the grave of Abner. 'And all the people took notice of it and it pleased them: as whatsoever the king did pleased all the people.'

This was because they loved their king. They

85

watched him, with admiration and love. They took notice of the kind and gracious things he did and said. The Pharisees didn't do that with the Lord Jesus, did they? They watched Jesus in order to find fault with him. Do you take notice of what your King Jesus does? Does it please you to hear and read what he did and is doing? You should be pleased if he really is your King.

But the 'whatsoever' is a little harder; and yet, if you really learn it, it makes everything easy. For if we learn to be pleased with whatsoever our King Jesus does we will not be disappointed with anything.

Suppose something comes today which is not quite what you would have liked: heavy rain, for instance, when you wanted to go out – remember that your King Jesus sent the rain and that will hush the little murmur and make you content. Ask him this morning to make you so loving and loyal to him, that *whatsoever* he does, all day long, may please you, because it has pleased him to do it. I think he loves us so much, that he always gives us as much happiness as he can possibly trust us with. He does what is most pleasant for his children whenever he sees it will not hurt them. So, when he does something which at first does not seem so pleasant you can still trust your King Jesus and learn by his grace to be pleased with *whatsoever* he does.

> *I hear a sweet voice ringing clear,*
> *All is well!*
> *It is my Father's voice I hear,*
> *All is well!*
> *Where'er I walk that voice is heard*
> *It is my God, my Father's Word —*
> *Fear not, but trust; I am the Lord,*
> *All is well.*

Our Comforter

'When the Comforter is come'
John 15.26

We can often want comforting. When something troubles you sometimes grown-up people do not know about it. Sometimes they don't think it is much to be troubled about. When nobody comforts you you can feel very sad. Sometimes they try, and yet it does not seem to work. And sometimes you have even 'refused to be comforted' because you feel so sad you don't want anyone to talk to you at all.

But then the Holy Spirit is called 'The Comforter!' What a beautiful name. It is so gentle, kind, loving. And he is true to his name. He brings comfort for our troubles.

Has he come to you? Your heavenly Father has promised to give the Holy Spirit to them that ask him. So, if you ask, he is sure to give. Then ask that the Holy Spirit may come into your heart, and dwell there always. Has he come to you? Perhaps you are not sure if he has or not? The rest of this verse tells you how you may know. Jesus said, 'When the Comforter is come, he shall testify of me.' That means, he will *tell you about Jesus*; he will put thoughts of Jesus into your mind, and love to Jesus into your heart, and he will make you see and understand more about Jesus than you did before. If you think about him, and try to please him, I think the Comforter has come, and is beginning to testify of Jesus in you.

Has he come to you? Then you will never be without a Comforter, whatever troubles come; if they are little disappointments, he can make you see the bright side, and be patient, and trustful and happy; if they are great troubles, perhaps illness, or even death, he can still comfort you, so that you will find out for the first time what a *very* precious gift he is, and what sweet peace can hush your sorrow when the Comforter is come.

Our blest Redeemer, ere he breathed
His tender, last farewell,
A Guide, a Comforter, bequeathed,
With us to dwell.

And his that gentle voice we hear,
Soft as the breath of even,
That checks each fault, that calms each fear,
And speaks of heaven.

The New Heart

'A new heart also will I give you.'
Ezekiel 36:26

Why does God promise this? It is because our old hearts are so evil that they cannot be made better. Nothing will do any good but giving us a completely new heart. Because we cannot make it for ourselves; the more we try, the more we shall find we cannot do it; so God, in his great pity and kindness, will give it us.

Because unless we have a new heart we cannot enter the kingdom of God, we cannot even see it! Without this gift we must be left outside in the terrible darkness when 'the door is shut.'

What is the difference? The old heart or the old self *likes* to be naughty in some way or other; either it likes to be lazy, or it likes to let out sharp words, or to go on being sulky or fretful instead of clearing up and saying, 'I am sorry!' The new heart *wants* to be good; and is upset when a temptation comes. The new heart does not wish to give into it; and would like to be always pleasing the Saviour.

The old heart is afraid of God and does not love him. The old heart wants to hide from God. It does not want God to see what it is doing. And it does not care to hear about Jesus, but would rather be let alone. The new heart loves God and trusts what he says and likes to know that he is always watching it. And it is glad to hear about Jesus and wants to come closer to him.

The old heart is a slave of Satan, taking his orders and doing what he wishes. The new heart is a happy servant of Christ, listening to his orders and doing what he wishes.

Oh how happy and blessed to have this new heart! All God's own children receive it, for he has said, 'I will give them one heart'; that is, all the same new heart. Do you not want to have it too? Then 'ask and you *shall* receive'; for he has said, 'A new heart also *will* I give you!'

> *Oh for a heart to praise my God,*
> *A heart from sin set free!*
> *A heart that always feels thy blood,*
> *So freely shed for me.*
> *A heart resigned, submissive, meek,*
> *My dear Redeemer's throne;*
> *Where only Christ is heard to speak,*
> *Where Jesus reigns alone.*

The Blind Man

'What do you want me to do for you?'
Luke 18.41.

There was only a blind beggar by the wayside but Jesus of Nazareth stood still when he cried to him. He could not find his way among the crowd, but Jesus commanded him to be brought near to him. He knew why the poor man had cried out, but Jesus wanted the blind man to come to him and tell him his problems by himself. So he said, 'What do you want me to do for you?' What a wonderful question, with a wonderful promise wrapped up in it! For it meant that the mighty Son of God was ready to do whatever this poor blind beggar asked. What did he ask? First of all he asked for what he most wanted! Not what he was supposed to ask for, nor what any had taught him to ask for, nor what other people asked; but simply *what he wanted*. Secondly, he asked straight off for a miracle! The blind man didn't stop and wonder whether it was likely to happen or not, nor how Jesus of Nazareth would do it, nor whether it was too much to ask all at once, nor whether the people would think he was rude asking for such a big thing. He knew what he wanted, and he believed that Jesus of Nazareth could do it, and so he asked, and that was enough.

And Jesus said to him, 'Receive your sight: your faith has saved you.'

And *that* was enough, his prayer of faith, and

Christ's answer of power, for 'immediately he received his sight.' Was that all? Did he go back to beg by the wayside? No, 'he followed him, glorifying God.' What a change from the cry of only a few minutes before!

Just one thing more is told us in this lovely little story, 'And all the people, when they saw it, gave praise to God.' See what that first cry of 'Have mercy on me,' led to! A few minutes before no one would have expected to have seen the poor blind man with his eyes open, following Jesus, glorifying God, and causing a whole crowd to praise him! Jesus says to you tonight, 'What do *you* want me to do for you?' What will you answer him?

> *Pass me no, O tender Saviour!*
> *Let me love and cling to thee;*
> *I am longing for thy favour,*
> *When thou comest, call for me.*
> *Even me.*

The Gift of the Holy Spirit

'I will put my Spirit within you.'
Ezekiel 36:27

Many years ago a man who loved God wrote a tiny prayer. It was so short that if anyone heard it they would remember it. God seemed to set that little prayer 'upon wheels,' so that it might run everywhere. It was printed on large cards and hung up and it was printed on small ones and kept in Bible and pocket books. It was taught to classes and schools and whole congregations and now thousands upon thousands pray it constantly. It is a prayer which must be heard, because it asks for what God has promised to give; and it asks for this through Jesus Christ - and God the Father hears him always. This is the prayer, 'O God, give me your Holy Spirit, for Jesus' Christ's sake. Amen.'

You should pray this prayer too. Begin this morning and go on, not just *saying* it, but *praying* it, till you get an answer. For you are quite sure to get it. Here is God's own promise, 'I *will* put my Spirit within you.' He has promised it over and over again in other places. Perhaps you will not know when the answer comes. Can you see the dew fall? No one ever saw a single drop come down and yet as soon as the sun rises, you see that it has come and is sparkling all over the fields. It came long before you saw it, falling sweetly and silently in the twilight and in the dark. So do not think that God is not hearing you because you have not felt anything very sudden and wonderful. He is hearing and answering all the time. You would not go on asking unless the dew of his Spirit were already falling upon your heart and teaching you to pray. The more he gives you of his blessed Spirit, the more you will ask for; and the more you ask, the more he will give.

Thou gift of Jesus, now descend,
And be my Comforter and Friend;
O Holy Spirit, fill my heart,
That I from Christ may ne'er depart

Show me my soul all black within,
and cleanse and keep me pure within;
Oh, show me Jesus! Let me rest
My heart upon his loving breast!

This same Jesus

'This same Jesus'
Acts 1:11

'Jesus Christ, is the same yesterday, and today, and forever.' Yes, he is the very same to you tonight that he was to the disciples who stood gazing up into heaven. After Jesus had lifted up his hands and blessed them, he went up to the opening gates of heaven – to glory. And he is the same Jesus now as he was then.

He is the very same to you tonight that he was to the little children, when he took them up in his arms and blessed them. Not a bit different! Just as kind, just as loving, just as ready to take you up too, and bless you, and keep you always 'safe in the arms of Jesus.'

The very same to you tonight that he was when he said so lovingly, 'Come to Me, all you that labour and are heavy laden, and I will give you rest.' I am sure that you feel that you would have loved Jesus ever so much if you had heard him say those words, and that you would have gone to him at once, because he was so good and kind! Well, he is this same Jesus now. When you lie down, see how many sweet and gracious words and deeds of his that you can remember. Say to yourself with every one, 'he is the same now, and the same for me!'

You are not always the same to him. When he comes and knocks at the door of your heart, you are sometimes ready to open; and sometimes you give him a cold, short, careless answer; and sometimes no answer at all. But he is always the same to you; always ready to receive you with tender love and forgiveness when you come to him.

Perhaps you do not feel so happy now as you did one day when you felt that he was very near and gracious, and full of forgiving love to you? What has changed? Only your feelings, not the Lord Jesus. He is always 'this same Jesus'; and you may rest on this tonight, and for ever.

For this word, O Lord, we bless thee,
For our Saviour's changeless name;
Yesterday, to-day, for ever,
Jesus Christ is still the same.

How to Conquer

'The Lord shall fight for you.'
Exodus 14:14

The Israelites were on the shores of the Red Sea but the Egyptians were marching after them. This made the Israelite people very frightened so they must have been very glad to hear Moses say 'The Lord will fight for you.'

The Egyptians had been cruel masters to them; and they had horses and chariots to pursue them with; and there was the sea close before them and no boats! Perhaps some thought it was no use. 'We will only be overtaken and conquered and be worse off than before.' And this would have happened if they had been on their own but God fought for them in a way they never thought of. For 'the Lord saved Israel that day out of the hand of the Egyptians and Israel saw the Egyptians dead upon the seashore.'

What about your Egyptians? – the angry tempers or sulky looks, impatient words, foolish thoughts, the sins that you keep doing, time and time again. Have you tried so often to fight these things and failed? Perhaps you have tried so hard that it seems no use and you do not know how you can conquer them or escape them? Are you tired of fighting and very afraid of always doing the wrong thing?

Now hear God's true, strong promise to you. 'The Lord shall fight for you!' 'Will he really?' Yes, really and he will conquer for you too, if you will only believe his Word and trust the battle to him and *let* him fight for you.

How? First, watch! And then the very instant you see the enemy coming, look up and say, 'Come, Lord and fight for me'; and keep *expecting* him to fight for you. And *you will find* that he does fight for you and gives you the victory; and you too will be 'saved that day'. Try him and trust him; and you, even you, will be 'more than conqueror through him that loved you.'

So when you meet with trials,
And know not what to do;
Just cast the care on Jesus,
And he will fight for you.
Gird on the heavenly armour
Of faith and hope and love;
And when the conflict's ended,
You'll reign with him above.

Come and see

'Come and see'
John 1:39, 46.

The Lord Jesus said it first. He said it to the two disciples of John who heard that he was the Lamb of God. They knew very little about him, but they followed him. Perhaps they were too nervous to speak, but 'Jesus turned, and saw them following,' and spoke to them. Then they asked him where he was living, and he said, 'Come and see!'

Philip said it next. He had found Christ himself,

and at once he told his friend Nathanael about him, and said, 'Come and see!'

These words are said to you tonight. Please 'come and see' Jesus! Come and kneel down before him, see what a glorious and loving Lord Jesus we have, and see what a lovely and precious Saviour he is! Come and see how kind and good he is! Come and see how ready he is to receive you, to take you up in his arms and bless you. Come and see what he has done for you; see how he loved you and gave himself for you; how he lived, and suffered, and bled, and died for you! Come and see what gifts he has for you, his grace, his joy and his love! Come and see where he lives – see that he is ready to come in and live with you, to make your little heart his own dwelling-place. Oh, if I could but persuade you to 'come and see!' There is no other sight so glorious and beautiful. Will you not come?

When you have come, when you can say like

107

Philip, 'We have found him!' and like Paul, 'We see Jesus,' will you not say to someone else, 'Come and see'? You will wish every one else to come to him. God's word tells you to try to bring them: 'Let him that hears say, Come!' Will you not say 'Come' to a friend or brother or sister, or to any one to whom Jesus makes you wish to say it? There is no sweeter invitation for you to give than 'Come and see Jesus!'

> *Jessie, if you only knew*
> *What he is to me,*
> *Surely you would love him too,*
> *You would 'come and see.'*
>
> *Come, and you will find it true,*
> *Happy you will be!*
> *Jesus says, and says to you,*
> *'Come! Oh come to me!'*

The Master's Voice

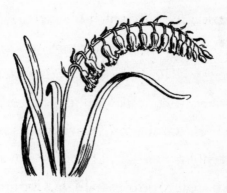

*'I will watch to see what he will
say to me.' Habakkuk 2:1*

When the Lord Jesus said to Simon the Pharisee,
'Simon, I have something to say to you'; he
answered, 'Master, say on!' When God was going
to speak to Samuel, he said, 'Speak, Lord, for
your servant is listening.' Has the Lord Jesus
said anything like this for us? He says, 'I have
yet many things to say to you.' What things?
They will be strong, helpful, life-giving words,
for he says, 'The words that I speak to you,

109

they are spirit and they are life.' They will be very loving words, for he says, 'I will speak comfortably to her', which means, 'I will speak to her heart, I will speak words of comfort.' And they will be very kind and tender words and spoken just at the right moment, for he says that he knows 'how to speak a word in season to him that is weary.'

'Will he really speak to me?' says the little heart. Yes, really. But what you have to do is wait to see what he will say to you. For it will be 'a still small voice,' and you will not hear it at all if you do not listen for it. 'How will he speak to me?' If I had something very nice to tell you, instead of saying it out loud, I could write it down on a piece of paper and gave that to you to look at. That would be exactly the same as if I had told it to you with my lips, wouldn't it? And you would take the paper eagerly to see what it was that I had to say to you. So today, when you read your Bible, either alone or at your Bible lesson, watch to see what Jesus will say to you in it. He always has something to say to you in his word. You will see something that you understand and that is helpful to you and that, perhaps, you never noticed much before. Please, listen lovingly to it, for *that* is what he says to you! Or if you are really longing for a word from him, some sweet text will come into your mind and you will wonder what made you think of it! That is the voice of Jesus speaking to your heart. Listen to it and treasure it up and follow it; and then watch to see what else he will say to you. Say to him, 'Master, say on!'

Master, speak! And make me ready,
When thy voice is truly heard,
With obedience glad and steady
Still to follow every word.
I am listening, Lord for thee;
Master, speak, oh speak to me!

Telling Jesus

'Told him all things'
Mark 6.30.

When you have been out for a day, what do you look forward to as you come home in the evening? Why do you run so eagerly into the house, and look so bright? You want to tell 'all about it' to someone whom you love - father or mother, or brothers and sisters; and you can hardly talk fast enough to pour it all out. You begin at the beginning, and tell everything (if they will only let you stay up long enough), the pleasures and the problems, what has been done, or what has been said.

When each day is over, and you go up to bed, what do you tell Jesus? Do you tell him everything too? Perhaps you do not tell him anything at all; or perhaps you only tell him of something that you have done wrong, and are sorry for. Have you ever thought of telling him *everything?* Jesus actually loves you *better* than your family who listened to all your news downstairs.

When the Apostles had been away, they 'gathered themselves together to meet Jesus, and told him all things, both what they had done, and what they had taught.' It is easy to picture the gentle, gracious Jesus listening to everything so kindly, so patiently, letting them tell him all their mistakes and all their success, all that had made them glad and all that had made them sorry. I am sure that you can picture the disciples sitting at Jesus' feet, and looking up into his face, and seeing how interested he was in all they had done, and not wishing to keep anything back from such a dear Master. They would have found their own love for Jesus growing warmer and brighter after this wonderful time of talking to him! It would have been so different if they had just said a few cold words to him, and never *told* him anything! How much better it is to tell Jesus everything! Try this tonight! It will be such a help and a comfort, and before long you too will find it such a joy to tell Jesus everything!

> *Tell him all the failures,*
> *Tell him all the sins;*
> *He is kindly listening*
> *Till his child begins.*

> *Tell him all the pleasures*
> *Of your merry day,*
> *Tell him all the treasures*
> *Crowning all your way.*

Who will take care of me?

'He cares for you.'
1 Peter 5:7

It is so pleasant to be cared for; to have kind relations and friends who show that they love you. They care about you and they care for you. What would you do if no one cared for you? There are children all over the world who are all alone without anyone to love them. These children have to look after themselves, even children that are younger than you are. What would you do if there was no one to get anything for you to eat, or to mend your clothes, or to keep a home for you to live in? What would you do if there was no one to take any notice if you hurt yourself, or if you were ill? If this was to happen to you, you would soon realise how important it is to have someone to care for you. But all the kindness and care that you have on earth comes to you because 'He cares for you.'

God planned and arranged everything so that you would be cared for. And you didn't have to do anything. He did not arrange it at the beginning of time, or at the beginning of your life and then just leave you and other people to get on with it. No! Every day, every moment, he cares, *goes on* caring, for you. Not only thinking of you and watching you, but working for you; making things come right, so that everything should be just the best that could happen to you. He doesn't just care about the big things and leave the little things to arrange themselves. God loves you and wants to look after the very small things that concern you. Even in some tiny little trouble, which no one else seems to care about, 'he cares'; or when everyone else is too busy with other things to listen to you, 'he cares for you.'

You can never get beyond God's care, for it always reaches you; you can never be outside of it, for it is always enfolding you.

'Who will take care of me?' darling, you say.
Lovingly, tenderly watched as you are!
Listen! I give you the answer today,
ONE who is never forgetful or far.

He will take care of you! All through the year
Crowning each day with his kindness and love,
Sending you blessings and shielding from fear,
Leading you on to his bright home above.

Christ's Death for us

'Our Lord Jesus Christ, who died for us'
1 Thessalonians 5: 9, 10.

Jesus died for us! Can you think of anyone else who did as much for you or loved you as much? No, you can't. Think what it really means, because it is really true; and it is horribly ungrateful to not even think about it.

It would be horrible to be punished for something that you didn't do; but this is exactly what happened to your dear Saviour. He let himself be punished for what you did.

Suppose some cruel man were going to cut off your leg, what would you think if your brother came and said, 'No, chop mine off instead!' But that would not be dying for you. And 'our Lord Jesus Christ *died*' for you.

It was the very most he could do, to show his very great love to you. Jesus didn't have to go through with it. He could have come down from the cross at any moment. The nails could not have kept him there for a moment longer than he chose; his love and pity were the real nails that held him fast to the cross till the very end, till he could say, 'It is finished,' till he '*died* for us.'

It was not only because he loved his Father that he did it. He also did it because he loved us. The text goes on to say 'Who died for us, that, whether we wake or sleep, we might live together with him.' So he loved us so much that he wanted us to live together with him; and as no sin can enter his holy and beautiful home, he knew our sins must be taken away before we could go there. And only blood could take away sin, only death could atone or make amends for it; and so he bled, that we might be washed in his most precious blood; he died, 'that, whether we wake or sleep, we might live together with him.'

There is a word I have to speak,
Jesus died!
O eyes that weep, and hearts that break,
Jesus died!
No music from the quivering string
Could such sweet sounds of rapture bring,
O may I always love to sing,
Jesus died! Jesus died!

Under his Wings

'Under his wings you shall trust.'
Psalm 61:4

That means today, not some other time! Under his wings, the shadowing wings of the Most High, you are to trust today.

When the little eaglets, that have not yet a feather to fly with, are under the great wings of the parent eagle, how safe they are! Who would dare touch them? If a bold climber put his hand into the nest then, those powerful wings would beat him in a minute. The bird would attack him and he may even loose his hold and fall. So just as the eaglet is safe under the wings of the eagle so you shall be safe with God. Because 'under his wings, nothing at all shall hurt you'.

If you are out on your own on the mountain side it can be dangerous if you are not properly clothed. But when the wild snowstorms rage round the eyrie[1] and the cold mountain air is felt the little eaglets are kept snug and warm! The small featherless things are protected from ice and wind and not a snowflake touches them. You shall also be kept warm 'under his wings,' when any cold day of trouble comes, or even any sudden blast of unkindness or loneliness.

'Under his wings you shall *trust!*'

Not 'you shall *see!*' What would happen to a little eaglet if it decided to go and see for itself what was going on. If the little bird thought it could take care of itself for a little while and hopped from under the shadow of the wings, it

1 Eagle's nest

would be neither safe nor warm. The sharp wind would chill it and a cruel hand might seize it. So you are to *trust*, rest quietly and peacefully, 'under his wings'. Stay there, and don't be peeping out and wondering whether God is really taking care of you! You will always be safe and happy with God. Safe, for 'in the shadow of your wings will I make my refuge.' Happy, for 'in the shadow of your wings will I rejoice.'

Remember, too, that it is a command as well as a promise; it is what you are to do today, all day long: 'Under his wings you *shall* trust!'

I am trusting thee, Lord Jesus, Trusting only thee.
Trusting thee for full salvation, Great and free.
I am trusting thee to guide me,
Thou alone shalt lead!
Every day and hour supplying
All my need.

Nothing, or Everything?

'Is it nothing to you?'
Lamentations 1.12.

This was said of a great, great sorrow, which should have touched the heart of every one who passed by and saw it, the terrible troubles that came upon the city Jerusalem and all the children and grown ups who lived there. But this sorrow was also a picture or type of the far more terrible sorrow which the Lord Jesus suffered willingly for us, so that we might receive his pleasures instead. Listen! It is as if he said to

124

you and me, 'Is it nothing to you, all you that pass by? Behold and see if there be any sorrow like my sorrow!'

'Behold and see' how all his life he was 'a Man of sorrows,' not having anywhere to lay his head; his own brothers refusing to believe in him, the wicked Jews hating him, and over and over again trying to kill him, and he knowing all the time what awful suffering was before him.

Look at him in the garden of Gethsemane, 'being in an agony,' and saying, 'My soul is very sorrowful, even to death.'

Look at him, whipped, scourged and spat upon, led like a lamb to the slaughter, and then nailed to the cross; suffering even to death, thirsting in the terrible pain, and yet not drinking to still it, and saying in the midst of it all, 'My God, my God, why have you forsaken me?' Was ever any sorrow like the sorrow that our Lord Jesus Christ went through for love of us? Is it nothing to you? Can you look at it and not care about it? Can you 'pass by' and go on just the same as if he had never loved and suffered?

Oh, instead of 'nothing,' let it, from this moment on, be *everything* to you! Let it be the reason why you hate sin and why you try to do right; let it be your peace and joy, your strength and your song; let it fill your heart with love and thankfulness; let it make you brave and determined to live for him who suffered and died for you.

> *See, oh see, what love the Saviour*
> *Also hath on us bestowed;*
> *How he bled for us and suffered,*
> *How he bare the heavy load.*
> *On the cross and in the garden*
> *Oh how sore was his distress!*
> *Is not this a love that passeth*
> *Aught that tongue can e'er express?*

Always Near

'I am with you always.'
Matthew 28:20

How nice it would be if we could always have the one we loved best in all the world with us; never away from us night or day and no fear that they ever possibly would or could leave us; never a goodbye and never, never the long farewell of death!

Can this ever be for you? Yes, it can. Jesus says 'I am with you always', to everyone who is his disciple (that is, who learns about him and makes him their Master). He does not say, 'I will be with you'; so that you might be wondering when he meant to come, when he would begin to be 'with you'; but he says, 'I *am* with you.' Jesus is with you, even now, though perhaps, like the two who walked with Jesus on the road to Emmaus, you don't realise it. Your feeling or not feeling that he is there has nothing at all to do with it, because his Word must be true and *is* true and he has said, 'I *am* with you always.' All you have to do is to be happy in believing it to be true. And if you go on believing it, you will soon begin to realize it; that is, to find that it is a real thing and that Jesus really is with you.

How long will he be with you? Always, 'all the days!' He has said, 'I will never leave you.' 'Never,' means really *never*, not for one moment. You cannot get through your life and all through God's great 'forever.' And 'always' means really *always*, every single moment of all your life, so that you need never ask again, 'Is Jesus with me now?' Of course he is! The answer will always be 'yes,' because he has said, 'I am with you always.' How safe, how sweet, how blessed!

> O Jesus, make thyself to me
> A living, bright reality!
> More present to faith's vision keen
> Than any outward object seen;
> More dear, more intimately nigh,
> Than even the sweetest earthly tie.

The Beauty of the Lord

'Yes, he is altogether lovely'
Song of Solomon 5:16

We do not need to ask who this verse is talking about – for these words could only be said of One, – the Beloved One, the Holy One, the Blessed One, the Glorious One! Only of Jesus, *our* Lord Jesus. Even though we haven't seen him face to face we still love him and one day we shall see him in all his beauty. On that day 'he shall come to be glorified in his saints, and to be admired in all them that believe!' Oh, if we could see Jesus now, as he is at this very moment, sitting at the right hand of the Majesty on high, the very brightness of God's glory, the splendour would be too great. Unless the Lord gave us the strength to be able to look at him and see his glory we would fall at his feet as though dead. But if Jesus laid his right hand upon us, saying, 'Fear not,' and we looked again, what would we see? We would see such loveliness and unspeaksable beauty! 'Fairer than the children of men,' and 'the chiefest among ten thousand,' is our Lord Jesus! And in all the glory he is 'this same Jesus'; although his appearance is now like the sun shining in his strength, there is the gentle smile for his children, and the tender kindness for the sick ones, and the wonderful, wonderful look of mighty love that would bring the whole world to Jesus if they could only see it. And there are scars too, which make his very beauty more beautiful, for they are scars of love

– the print of the nails which he bore for us on the Cross. The angels and redeemed ones around him can see them even now; for even 'in the midst of the throne' he is the 'Lamb, as it had been slain.' So the love has overflowed the glory, and our Lord Jesus is 'altogether lovely.' *Our* Lord Jesus! Yes, for the Altogether Lovely One has given himself for us, and given himself to us; so that even the least of his little ones may look up and say, 'This is my Beloved, and this is my Friend!'

> *Oh Saviour, precious Saviour,*
> *My heart is at thy feet;*
> *I bless thee, and I love thee,*
> *And thee I long to meet.*

> *To see thee in thy beauty,*
> *To see thee face to face,*
> *To see thee in thy glory,*
> *And reap thy smile of grace!*

Doing God's Will

'Teach me to do your will.'
Psalm 143:10

Have you ever thought when you see someone enjoying themselves doing a beautiful and pleasant piece of work, 'I should like to be able to do that!' and perhaps you have said, 'Please, teach me how to do it.'

Can you think of anything more pleasant to do than what the angels are doing? And as they do it they are full of delight. Can you think of anything more beautiful to do than what is done

133

in heaven – the beautiful home above? Is there anything more interesting to do there? Those who live there will never get tired of doing this for thousands of millions of years. Would you not like to be taught to do it too? To begin the pleasant, beautiful and most interesting work now, instead of waiting till you are grown up? If you wait until then perhaps you will never learn it all, because you put it off? Well if you want to learn this wonderful work then pray this little prayer this morning with all your heart, 'Teach me to do your will.' For it is his will that is the happiest work above and the very happiest thing to do here below.

What is his will? The Prayer-Book version of this Psalm tells you very simply and sweetly. It says, 'Teach me to do the thing that pleases you.' So doing God's will is just doing the things, one by one, that please him.

Why did David ask this? He goes on to say

why – 'For you are my God.' If God is really *our* God we shall wish to do the thing that pleases him. David did not think he could do it himself, for he says next, 'Let your loving Spirit lead me.' His loving Spirit will lead you too and show you how beautiful and grand God's will is. He will make you long to do it always and teach you to do it. So that even on earth you may begin to do what the angels are doing in heaven!

It is but very little
For him that I can do,
Then let me seek to serve him,
My earthly journey through;
And without sigh or murmur,
To do his holy will;
And in my daily duties
His wise commands fulfil.

Jesus Will Return

'Behold, he comes!'
Revelation 1:7

Are you wondering why this verse has been chosen tonight? Look at it again: '*he* comes!' Who? Jesus himself, the 'same Jesus' who said, 'Come to Me.' You thought it would be so nice to come to Jesus, if you could only see him. But you will see him, for he is coming.

Think of seeing the Lord Jesus, so beautiful, so glorious, so 'altogether lovely.' Think about how you will see him, the very same dear, kind

Saviour, who loves children, who loves you and has called you! You will see his face; the brow that was crowned with thorns, the eyes that looked on Peter, the lips that said such wonderful and gracious things! You will no longer just think about him, and try to believe in him, and pray to him, and wish for him, but really see him! Isn't this something to look forward to very much?

Only one thing would make it terrible, and that is, if you will not come to him now, and will not let him wash away your sins in his precious blood. Then it would indeed be terrible, for he would never say to you any more 'Come!' but only 'Depart!'

But you want him to wash you clean, do you not? And you did try to come to him? And you believe he means what he says, and really died to save you? Then, you shall be very glad to see him! What if now you heard the cry, 'Jesus is coming!' Your heart would beat quick, but I think it would be with gladness, not with terror. If you heard the call, 'Jesus is coming!' Would you not run out to meet him? Jesus is coming! Could anything be happier news? We probably won't think much about the sound of the trumpet, and the clouds of glory, and all the holy angels that will be arriving with him. It will just be Jesus that we really want to see. And then we shall hear his own voice, and that will fill our eyes and our hearts for ever.

Thou art coming, O my Saviour!
Thou art coming, O my King!
In thy beauty all-resplendent,
In thy glory all-transendent,
Well may we rejoice and sing!

Working for Jesus

'Ye have done it to me.'
'Ye did it not to me.' Matthew 25:40 & 45

Our Lord Jesus Christ has given us opportunities to show if we love him or not. He tells us that what we try to do for anyone who is poor, or hungry, or sick, or a lonely stranger, is just the same as doing it to him. And when he says, 'Come, you who are blessed,' he will remember these little things and will say, 'You have done it to me.' But he tells us that if we do nothing for them, it is just the

139

same as if he were standing there and we would do nothing for him. And he will say, 'You did it not to me.'

He will say one thing or the other to you on that great day when you see Jesus the King on the throne of his glory. Which shall it be? What are you doing for Jesus? Are you doing anything? Perhaps you say, 'There is nothing that I can do.' Have you ever tried to find something to do for Jesus? Have you ever asked him to give you an opportunity to do something for him? Or have nyou ever cared or tried to do anything for him? Be honest. He knows and will forgive.

But now, what is to be done? Begin by asking him to show you. Keep a bright, sharp lookout and see if you can find an opportunity very soon (and perhaps many) of doing something kind for Jesus' sake. It may be that you will be able to help a poor or sick or lonely one. Think hard about what you could do!

It is actually very kind of the Lord Jesus to have told us this. For he knew that those who really love him would *want* to do something for him. But the problem is what can we do for Jesus the King of Glory who lives in his glorious heaven? So it was wonderfully thoughtful of him to give us opportunities to show love and care for others. And it was good of Jesus to tell us that, if we have only been kind to a sick old woman or hungry child, 'you have done it to me!'

> *I love my precious Saviour*
> *Because he died for me;*
> *And if I did not serve him,*
> *How sinful I should be!*
> *God help me to be useful*
> *In all I do or say!*
> *I mean to work for Jesus,*
> *The Bible says I may!*

My King!

'Now then do it'
2 Samuel 3:18

David had been anointed king over Israel long before, but the people did not make David their King while Saul was on the throne. Then after long wars and troubles Saul was killed. But still it was only Judah who followed David; and for seven years and a half Israel held back. At last Abner said to the elders of Israel, 'In the past you looked for David to be king over you. *Now then do it!*' And they did it.

Now God has, long ago, anointed the Lord Jesus to be our King, but is he your own King yet? Is he reigning in your heart? Have you ever come to him and said, 'You shall be *my* King, Lord Jesus'?

Perhaps in the past, like the Israelites, you wanted Jesus to be your King. Perhaps now you have been longing that he would come and stop all the wrong tempers and naughty thoughts which you have to struggle with. Do you really wish it? Then that wish is like a messenger sent to prepare the way before him; but wishing is not enough – 'Now then *do* it!' Now, this very night, before you go to sleep, tell the dear Saviour, who has been waiting, to come and set up his kingdom of peace and joy in your heart, that he shall be your King *now*! Make him your King at once; say to him reverently, and lovingly, and with all your heart, 'Jesus, my King!'

Then, when Satan tries to get back to his old

throne in your heart, tell him it cannot be his ever again, for you have given it to your King, Jesus, and that he is to reign there always; and that Jesus will not give it up, but will fight for you and help you fight against sin.

Do not say, 'Oh, yes, I should like this very much!' and just go to sleep as usual; but *do* it now! Then lie down with the happy thought, 'My King!'

> *Reign over me, Lord Jesus!*
> *Oh make my heart thy throne!*
> *It shall be thine, dear Saviour,*
> *It shall be thine alone.*

> *'Oh come and reign, Lord Jesus;*
> *Rule over everything!*
> *And keep me always loyal,*
> *And true to thee, my King!*

Standard Bearers

*'You have given a banner to them that
fear you.' Psalm 60:4*

What is your banner and what are you doing
with it? For if you are among 'them that fear'
God, he has given you a banner 'that it may be
displayed.' Is your banner furled up and put away
in a corner, so that nobody sees it or knows of
it? Or are you trying to be a brave standard bearer
of Jesus Christ, carrying his flag. I think the
motto on this flag is 'Love.' For we are told that
his banner over us is Love. Are you displaying it,

showing your love to him by your love to others? Showing the power of his love over you by your sweet, happy temper and by trying to please him always?

Carrying a banner means something. First, it means that you belong to or work for those whose banner you carry and that you are not ashamed of them. At big school festivals we know to which school a boy belongs by the flag that he carries or the uniform that he wears. You would like to carry the flag of your country, because you belong to it and are loyal. So let us carry the banner of Jesus Christ because we are loyal to him and are not ashamed to own him as our King.

Secondly, it means that we are ready to fight and ready to encourage others to fight under the same banner. When you are tempted to do something wrong, remember whose banner you carry and do not disgrace it. If one does right, it makes it easier for the others to do right too.

Thirdly, it means rejoicing. You know how flags are hung out on festival days and carried in triumphant processions. The hand that carries Christ's banner through his war, will carry it also in his triumph; the hand that tries to unfurl it bravely now, will wave it when his glorious reign begins and his blessed kingdom is come. Then, 'in the name of our God we will set up our banners' *now!*

What is your banner? How do you raise it up and show it to others? Tell people about the Lord Jesus and how wonderful he is. Don't be quiet. Don't hide the truth - tell people about it.

The Master hath called us,
the children who fear him,
Who March 'neath Christ's banner,
his own little band;
We love him and seek him;
we long to be near him,
And rest in the light of his beautiful land.

Called by Name

'I have called you by your name'
Isaiah 43:1

Look out, if it is a clear night, and see the stars sparkling all over the sky. You cannot count them; no one can, because there are more than eyes or telescopes have ever reached. But 'God calls them all by names.' He knows every one separately. And yet, though he has all those wonderful worlds of light in his hands, and 'brings out their host by number,' he turns to say to each of his weak children on this dark earth, 'I have called you by your name.'

He knows your name; you are not just one of the rest to him, you are known by name to him. Say aloud your own name – Jesus knows this name also!

That name was given you in his presence, and by his minister, when you were baptized, in obedience to our Saviour's command. God knows it, and calls you by it.

But he has done more than this. Why do you read this little book every night? Why do you want to hear about Jesus, and salvation, and heaven? What is it that seems like a little voice inside, persuading you to seek and love Jesus?

That is God's own voice in your heart, calling you by name! For you know it is to *you*, because it is only in your own heart; no one else even knows of it.

When he calls like this, listen, and see what else he has to say to you: 'Fear not; for I have redeemed you, I have called you by your name; you are mine!'

> *Jesus is our Shepherd,*
> *For the sheep he bled;*
> *Every lamb is sprinkled*
> *With the blood he shed.*
>
> *Then on each he setteth*
> *His own secret sign;*
> *'They that have my Spirit,*
> *These,' saith he, 'are mine.'*

Soldiers

'Chosen to be a soldier.'
2 Timothy 2:4

Are you a soldier? You should be, for you have been chosen to be a soldier in the glorious army of Jesus Christ.

You should be, for you have been 'received into the congregation of Christ's flock' at your baptism. You have been enrolled to fight under Christ's banner against sin, the world and the devil. You have been enlisted to continue as Christ's faithful soldier and servant until your

151

life's end. You can never undo that, even if you are a deserter and found in the enemy's ranks. The Captain of our salvation will not undo it, if you will only come and enlist now. This very morning ask Jesus to receive you into his noble army and to give you, first, the shield of his salvation and then the whole armour of God and to teach you how to fight sin and the Devil and to give you victories every day. He will then let you share his grand triumphs afterwards.

Perhaps you have enlisted already? Perhaps you know that you love your Captain Jesus and he is helping you to fight the good fight of faith? What made you enlist? Was it because you were so brave and wonderful? Oh no! It was all because of Jesus. He chose you to be a soldier. You did not chose him to be a Captain. And then in the end it was the beautiful call of his love which persuaded you to join his ranks.

Now he fights not only beside you, and with you, but for you. In his war 'nothing shall by any means hurt you,' for 'he was wounded' for you. Your life is safe with him, for he laid down his own for you. By his side you can never be defeated, because he goes forth 'always conquering and to conquer.'

> *Stand up, stand up for Jesus!*
> *Ye soldiers of the cross;*
> *Lift high his royal banner,*
> *It must not suffer loss.*

> *From victory to victory*
> *His army shall be led,*
> *Till every foe is vanquished,*
> *And Christ is Lord indeed.*

> *Stand up, stand up for Jesus!*
> *The trumpet call obey;*
> *Forth to the mighty conflict.*
> *In this his glorious day!*

My Jewels

'That day when I make up my jewels'
Malachi 3:17

'My jewels!' God tells us who they are – 'Every one who fears the Lord, and thinks upon his name.' So if you fear the Lord, and think upon his name, you are one of his jewels, and all that you are going to read about them is for you, and means *you*.

'My jewels!' They are his 'special treasure.' His very own, dearer than all other treasures to him. We see how very precious they are to him by the price he paid for them. For every one of them has been purchased, not with silver and gold (all the silver and gold in the world would not have been enough to purchase one of them), but with the precious blood of Christ. That was the greatest thing God had to give, and he gave it for them.

God has found and chosen his jewels, and he will never lose them. Every one is kept safe in the casket of his everlasting love. He does not mean to hide them away, and be ashamed of them; for he says they shall 'be a crown of glory in the hand of the Lord, and a royal diadem in the hand of your God.' They are not all the same, jewels are of many different colours and sizes; but the day is coming when he will make them up, when they will all be gathered in his treasury, and shine in his glorious crown. Not one will be forgotten, or overlooked, or lost, for every one is 'precious in his sight.'

Is it not a grand thing to be one of God's jewels? How very wonderful that he should give such a beautiful name to his poor, sinful, worthless children, and set such shining hopes before them! Should we not to try to walk worthy of this high and holy calling?

Sons of Zion, ye are precious
In your heavenly Father's sight;
Ye are his peculiar treasure,
And his jewels of delight.

Sought and chosen, cleansed and polished,
Purchased with transendent cost,
Kept in his own royal casket,
Never, never to be lost.

A Loyal Aim

*'That he may please him who has chosen him
to be a soldier.'* 2 Timothy 2:4

Here is something worth aiming at, worth trying
for! The Lord Jesus, the Captain of our salvation,
is the one who has chosen us to be his soldiers;
and now, does he only tell us to do our duty – to
serve, obey and fight? No, he tells us something
more. He gives us a hope and an aim so bright
and pleasant, that it is like sunshine upon
everything. He says, we 'may *please* him.'

Only one who knows what it is to be sad

because they have upset the dear Saviour, can really understand what a happy request this is! Isn't it wonderful that we are told that we can actually please Jesus. Even after we were cold and careless and sinful. Even after we ignored Jesus' love for us over and over again! Oh, if we love him, our hearts will just leap at the hope of it! Perhaps we thought that we would never be able to please God until we reached heaven. But if you read God's word you will see that it says, we 'may please him' now, while we are soldiers, in the very midst of the fighting. Paul tells us one thing in which you may please God: 'Children, obey your parents in all things, for this really pleases the Lord.'

Shall this be your aim and your hope today? Look up to the Lord Jesus now and ask him first to give you the faith. Without this faith 'it is impossible to please God.' Then ask him to show you 'how you should walk and please

God.' Ask Jesus to help you to 'do those things that are pleasing in his sight'; that all your ways, even every step of your ways, may really and truly 'please the Lord' (Proverbs 16:7).

True-hearted, whole-hearted, faithful and loyal,
King of our lives, by they grace we will be;
Under thy standard, exalted and royal,
Strong in thy strength, we will battle for thee.

True-hearted, whole-hearted!
Fullest allegiance,
Yielding henceforth to our glorious King,
Valiant endeavour and loving obedience,
Freely and joyously now we would bring.

Always More!

'He gives more grace'
James 4:6

Yes, God always has more! And if he has given any at all, it is a certain proof that he will give more; for over and over again the Lord Jesus said, 'Whosoever has, to him shall be given.' So, if he has given you a little grace, just enough to wish for more, you shall have more, and then when he has given you more, that will be the very reason why you may expect more still. Is it not nice to be always looking forward to more grace? Then, as you grow older, and the little vessel grows larger, he will keep on pouring more grace into it. You will outgrow many things, but you will never outgrow this rich and precious supply.

'He gives more grace' than we ask. If he had given us only what we asked, we should never have had any at all, for it is his grace that first of all makes us wish, and teaches us to ask for it. And he says, 'Open your mouth wide, and I will fill it.' Then open it wide! Ask him to fill you with his grace.

'He gives more grace' than all our need. It never runs short. Whatever our need is, there is always enough grace for it, and then 'more' too! *always* more. If our need seems to become greater, we shall find the grace greater too, if we will only go to him who gives it; if the enemies that we are trying to fight against seem stronger than ever, we shall certainly find his grace stronger too, if we will only ask it, and take it, and use it.

We can never overtake this promise, much less outrun it; for however little we have, or however much we want, now this moment, and on to the end of our lives, it is always, always, 'He gives *more* grace!'

> *Have you in the Lord believed?*
> *Still there's more to follow;*
> *Of his grace have you received?*
> *Still there's more to follow.*
> *Oh the grace the Father shows!*
> *Still there's more to follow;*
> *Freely he his grace bestows,*
> *Still there's more to follow.*
>
> *More and more! more and more!*
> *Always more to follow!*
> *Oh his matchless, boundless love!*
> *Still there's more to follow!*

Obedience to Christ

'Whatsoever he saith to you, do it.'
John 2:5

How are you to know what Jesus says to you?
He has spoken so plainly to us in his Word! In
that he tells everyone exactly what to do. It is
wonderful how he has said everything there for
us, told us everything we should do. When you
read a chapter or hear one read, listen and watch
to see what he says to you in it. There is another
way in which he tells us what to do. Do you hear
a little voice inside that always tells you to do the

163

right thing and not to do the wrong thing? That is a conscience and God speaks to you by it.

Another way he speaks to you is through other people that he has put in charge of you. He has told you to 'obey your parents', and to 'obey them that rule over you.' So, when they tell you to do something, it is the Lord Jesus himself that you are obeying when you obey them.

Now 'whatsoever he says to you, do it!' Yes, 'whatsoever.' This means everything that he tells you whether it is easy or hard. You must do it because he tells you; do it for love of him and it will be a thousand times better and happier to obey your King Jesus than to please yourself. And he himself will help you to do it. All that you have to do is to look up to him for grace to obey and he will give it.

'Whatsoever he says to you, *do* it.' Do not just think about doing it, or talk about doing it, but *do* it! 'Do *it*!' Do the exact thing he would have you do, not something a little bit different or something which you think will be very nearly the same, but do '*it*.'

And 'do it' at once. It is so true, that the very first moment is the easiest for obedience. Every minute that you put off doing the right thing makes it harder. Do not let Jesus your King have to speak twice to you. 'Whatsoever he says to you, do it' cheerfully, exactly and instantly.

Jesus, help me, I am weak;
Let me put my trust in thee;
Teach me how and what to speak;
Loving Saviour, care for me,
Dear Saviour, hear me,
Hear a little child today;
Hear, oh hear me;
Hear me when I pray.

Satisfied

'Shall never thirst'
John 4:14

When you have had a treat or a pleasure, do you begin to wish for another? When you look over your playthings or your books (whichever you happen to care most for), have you not said, 'If I only had just this, or just that as well'? And even some children who seem to have everything and hardly know what to wish for, do not seem to have enough to make them *completely* happy. They still want something, without knowing what they want. Is not this something like feeling thirsty?

And when you get the very thing you most wanted, it does not make much difference, for very soon you want something else. This is just like being 'thirsty' again.

The Lord Jesus knows all about this, and so he said, 'Whosoever drinks of this water shall thirst again; but whosoever drinks of the water that I shall give him, shall never thirst.' The first thing that you must learn is that you always get thirsty again. It is no use expecting to find anything on this earth that will satisfy you for ever. But the second thing to learn is that Jesus has something to give you which will make you *completely* satisfied and glad. And as long as you go on drinking this, you will *always* be satisfied and glad. However, the third thing is that you cannot get this gladness from anyone or anything else. Jesus gives it, and Jesus only. And the fourth thing is that this gladness must be meant for you, because he says 'whosoever' and that means 'anybody that likes!' And he says, 'Ho, every one that thirsts, come to the waters!' And, 'If any man thirst, let him come to me and drink.' And, 'I will give to him that is thirsty water from the fountain of life freely.'

Will you not say to him, like the poor woman at the well, 'Lord Jesus, give me this water, that I thirst not!' Listen to his kind answer! 'Drink, drink abundantly, O beloved!'

I heard the voice of Jesus say,
Behold, I freely give
The living water; thirsty one,
Stoop down, and drink, and live.

I came to Jesus, and I drank
Of that life-giving stream;
My thirst was quenched, my soul revived,
And now I live in him.

Do it Heartily

'Whatsoever you do, do it heartily, as to the Lord.'
Colossians 3:23

In 2 Chronicles 31:21, we read of Hezekiah, 'in
every work that he began, he did it with all his
heart and prospered.' And this morning's verse
rings a New Testament echo, 'Do it heartily!' Sing
it now, like a little peal of bells!

'Do it heartily!'

See if that does not ring in your ears all day
and remind you that it is not just pleasanter to
be bright and brisk about everything, but that

it is actually one of God's commands, written in his own Word.

I know this is easier to some than to others. Perhaps it 'comes natural' to you to do everything heartily. That is very nice, but it is not enough. What else? 'Whatsoever you do, do it heartily, *as to the Lord* and not to men.' He knows if the hard working, energetic boy or girl wants to please him. He knows if they long to make him smile; or whether they have forgotten about him. He knows if they only care about the smile of others and the pleasure of being quick and busy. But perhaps it is hard for you to do things heartily. You like better to take your time and so you dawdle and do things in a lazy way, especially when it is something that you don't want to do. Is this right? Is it a little sin, when God's Word says 'Whatsoever you do, do it heartily?' Is it not just as much disobeying God as breaking any other command? Are you not *guilty* before him? Very likely you never thought of it in this way, but there the words stand and neither you nor I can alter them. First ask him to forgive you all the past idleness and lazy ways, for Christ's sake and then ask him to give you strength from now on to obey this Word of his. And then listen to the little chime, 'Do it heartily, do it heartily!' And *then* the last word of the verse about Hezekiah will be true of you too – 'Prospered!'

> *Up and doing, little Christian!*
> *Up and doing, while 'tis day!*
> *Do the work the Master gives you,*
> *Do not loiter by the way.*
> *For we all have work before us,*
> *You, dear child, as well as I;*
> *Let us learn to seek our duty,*
> *And to 'do it heartily'.*

Our Surety

'I will be surety for him'
Genesis 43:9

Judah, the elder brother, promised his father to bring Benjamin safely back from Egypt. He would be completely responsible for him. He would be the 'surety' or a guarantee for Benjamin. He said, 'If I do not bring him to you, and do not set him before you, then let me bear the blame for ever.' His father trusted Judah to do as he had said, and so Judah was the 'surety' or guarantee for Benjamin.

Jesus Christ is Surety for us. He, our Elder Brother, promises to bring us safely to the house of his Father and our Father. He promises to present us before the presence of his glory. We are in his hand, and from his hand God will require us and receive us. And God, who so loves his children, has trusted the Lord Jesus to do this. He has given us to him, and he has accepted Jesus Christ as our Surety. Jesus is the guarantee given to God that his children will be brought back to him safely.

Now, if God has trusted Jesus, will you not trust him too? Why would you hesitate to trust in Jesus? Who else can you trust? Who else could promise to bring you safe to heaven? Benjamin might possibly have found his way by himself from Egypt to Canaan; but never, never could you find the way by yourself from earth to heaven; and never, never could anyone but the Lord Jesus bring you there.

Benjamin could not be certain that his brother could keep his promise, for Judah was only a man, and might have been killed in Egypt. But you can be certain that your Elder Brother Jesus *can* keep his promise, for he is God as well as man. Do you think he *would* break his promise? He, the faithful Saviour, break his promise? Heaven and earth shall pass away, but his word shall not pass away! Then trust him now, and never sin against his faithful love again by not trusting him. He is our Surety. He is our guarantee and he will bring every one who trusts him safe to heaven.

Jesus, I will trust thee,
Trust thee with my soul!
Guilty, lost, and helpless,
Thou canst make me whole!
Jesus, I do trust thee,
Trust without a doubt!
Whosoever cometh,
Thou wilt not cast out.

The Sight of Faith

'As seeing him who is invisible.'
Hebrews 11:27

If we were always doing everything just as if we saw Jesus, how different our lives would be! We may not have seen Jesus face to face yet, but we still love him. And if we behaved as though we could see him everywhere how much happier our lives would be too! How brave and bright and patient we should be, if all the time we could really see Jesus as Stephen saw him! And by faith, the precious faith which God is ready to give to all who ask, we may go on our way with this light upon it, 'as seeing him who is invisible.'

These words were said about Moses. Seeing God by faith had three effects on him. First, 'he left Egypt.' These words made Moses ready to give up anything for his God and God's people. It made him true and loyal to God's cause. He did not care for anything else, so long as he saw God. Secondly, it took away all his fear. The wrath of the king meant nothing to him, when Jehovah was by his side. Of what should he be afraid? Thirdly, it helped him to wait patiently for forty years in the desert and work patiently for another forty years in the wilderness. Think how strength-giving that sight of faith must have been which helped him to endure everything for eighty years!

Try this for yourself. Ask God, before you go downstairs, for faith, so that you may walk all day long 'as seeing him who is invisible.' When you

are tempted to indulge in something wrong –
idleness or carelessness, or selfishness – this will
help you to give it up at once. You won't be able
to give into sin when you look into the eye of
Jesus. When something makes you afraid, this will
make you brave and peaceful. How can you fear
anything when your God is so near? When lessons,
or work, or even having to be quiet with nothing
to do, seem very tiresome and you are tempted to
be impatient and perhaps cross, this will help you
to feel patient; for how can you be impatient when
you are looking up to Jesus and he is looking down
on you all the time!

God will not leave me all alone,
He never will forsake his own;
When not another friend I see,
The Lord is looking down on me.

Our Forerunner

'He shall go over before.'
Deuteronomy 3:28

Joshua is a person in the Bible who in an interesting way teaches us about what Christ is like. There are others like this in the Bible and they are all called 'types' of Christ because they teach us a great deal about the Saviour.

God made Joshua to be 'a leader and commander of the people.' He was their captain in war, and their saviour from their enemies.

In this verse God told Moses that Joshua

should go into Canaan first before the people did, and 'cause them to inherit the land.'

This is what the Lord Jesus Christ has done for us. He has gone in front of the great army of the living God who have crossed or have yet to cross the river of death. His blessed feet have passed that river, and made the crossing easy for us, so that the dark waters shall never overflow one of us, not even a little child.

He has gone before us into the beautiful land. He has made everything ready. He is there, waiting for us. He will give us his own most sweet and gracious welcome to his own fair country, as soon as our feet have crossed the river.

Are you afraid to go to where Jesus is? You know you must die. Even little children die. You probably do not like to think about dying. But you don't need to think at all about lying cold and dead in a grave. When that does come, it will not matter to you in the least. If Jesus is your Saviour, he takes away your sins, and death will be like being carried in a minute across a narrow stream, and meeting your loving Jesus on the other side. But there is something else — Jesus will also come and fetch you himself and he will 'cause you to inherit' the wonderful land that he will take you too, so that it will be your own land, your own beautiful and holy and glorious home for ever.

Praying for his children,
In that blessed place,
Calling them to glory,
Sending them his grace;

'His bright home preparing,
Little ones, for you;
Jesus ever liveth,
Ever loveth too.

No Weights

'Let us lay aside every weight.'
Hebrews 12:1

If you were going to run a race, you would first put down all the parcels you were carrying. If you had a heavy little parcel in your pocket, you would lay it down too, because it would really slow you down. You certainly wouldn't say, 'I will put down the parcels which I have in my hands, but nobody can see the one in my pocket, so that one won't matter!' You would 'lay aside *every* weight.' Did you know that you have a race to run today? A little piece of a great race. God has given a splendid prize, 'the prize of the high calling of God in Christ Jesus,' a crown that is incorruptible.

Now what are you going to do about the weights that slow you down? Some things do seem to get in the way. Will you keep them or lay them aside? Are you just going to lay aside something that everyone can see is slowing you down, so that people will praise you for that? Then are you going to keep something that you know will stop you running the race and pleasing God though no one else knows anything at all about it? Take Paul's wise and holy advice, and make up your mind to lay aside *every* weight.

Different persons have different weights; we must find out what ours are and don't give up. Perhaps you find in the morning that you don't get up as soon as you are told. Then you will find that time slips by and there is not enough left for quiet prayer and Bible reading. Then here is a little weight that must be laid aside. Perhaps when you are at school there is a boy or girl and they persuade you to do wrong things. Then you must lay that weight aside. Perhaps when you go to bed you read a storybook - perhaps you read it so much that when it is time to say your prayers your head is so full of story that you only *say words* when you pray and you don't really *pray* at all. This is certainly a weight which must be laid aside!

It may seem hard to lay your favourite weight down; but if you only knew how light we feel when it is laid down and how much easier it is to run the race which God has set before us!

Oh Let my footsteps in thy word
aright still ordered be:
Let no iniquity obtain
dominion over me.
Psalm 119:133

Pleasures for Evermore

'At your right hand are pleasures for evermore.'
Psalm 16:11

You have never had a pleasure that lasted. You look forward to a great pleasure. It comes, and very soon it is gone. You can only look back on it. The longest and best day you ever had came to an end, and you had to go to bed and it was over. How different are the pleasures at God's right hand! They are for ever, and you cannot get to the end or see to the end of 'ever,' for there is no end to it.

You see it is not one pleasure only, but *'pleasures,'* lots and lots of them as they are unending. Do you wonder what they will be? We cannot even guess at most of them. If we think of the brightest and the best thing possible, we should still find, when we reached heaven, that God's 'pleasures' were much greater and better than we thought.

We can tell a few things about them. They will be holy pleasures, never mixed with any sin. They will be perfect pleasures, with nothing whatever to spoil them. They will be lasting pleasures, for tonight's text says so. They will be abundant pleasures, as many as we can possibly wish, for David says (Psalm 36:8), 'They shall be *abundantly satisfied* and you shall make them drink of the river of your pleasures.' They will be always freshly-flowing pleasures, for they are a river, not a little pool. They will be pleasures given by God himself to us, for it does not say

'they shall drink,' but '*you* shall *make them* drink of the river of *your* pleasures.'

And all these 'God has prepared' for you. Is he not good and kind!

Angel voices sweetly singing,
Echoes through the blue dome ringing,
News of wondrous gladness bringing,
Ah, 'tis heaven at last!

Not a tear-drop ever falleth,
Not a pleasure ever palleth,
Song to song for ever calleth;
Ah, 'tis heaven at last.

The Shield of Salvation

'You have also given me the shield of your salvation.'
1 Samuel 22:36

This beautiful little text teaches us a very precious truth. It shows us that the salvation, which the Lord Jesus came to bring, is not only salvation for the very last moment, just escaping hell, but that it is salvation now and salvation is everything. Salvation does not only mean victory at the last day, but it is like a broad shining shield, given to us in the middle of a battle, coming between us and the poisoned arrows and sharp

sword-thrust of the enemy. It is a shield not only to keep us from death, but to keep us from being hurt and wounded. It is the shield which Jesus, our Captain *has* given us to use now, as well as the crown which he *will* give when the warfare is ended.

How are you to use this shield? What does it really mean for you? It means, that if you have come to the Lord Jesus to be saved, he does not just say he *will* save you, but that you *are* saved, that he saves you now. And this is how you are to use it – believe it, and be sure of it, because you have his word for it; and then, when a temptation comes, tell the enemy that he has nothing to do with you, for you are saved; that you belong to Jesus and not to him – look up and say, 'Jesus saves me!' Will he fail you? Did he, did anyone ever find that they had been lied to by Jesus or that they were mistaken to believe in him and trust in his great salvation? Never! And never will you find this shield

of his salvation fail to cover you completely. Satan himself cannot touch you when you are behind this shield! Lift it up when you see him coming, even ever so far off and you will be safe.

> *Jesus saves me every day,*
> *Jesus saves me every night;*
> *Jesus saves me all the way,*
> *Through the darkness,*
> *through the light.*

The Great Promise

'This is the promise that he has promised us,
even eternal life.' 1 John 2:25

As the gift of the Holy Spirit was specially 'the promise of the Father,' so it seems that the gift of eternal life was specially the promise of the Lord Jesus. If you look in the Gospel of John, you will find that he promised Salvation not only once or twice, but fifteen times! So no wonder John in his Epistle calls it '*the* promise which he has promised us.'

If you made me a promise, even if you said

it only once, you would expect me to believe it, would you not? And you would be annoyed and hurt if I would not believe it. It would seem as if I thought you were not speaking the truth. And suppose I did not say whether I believed it or not, but simply took no notice at all of what you said, would that not be just as bad?

Now when the Lord Jesus himself has made us a great promise, surely he expects us to believe it? It must hurt him more than anything when we will not believe his kind words. And it seems almost worse when we do not take any notice of them, but go on just the same as if he had never promised anything at all.

So you see it is not only that you *may* believe this great promise of the Lord Jesus, but that you *should* believe it, and that you are wronging his love and upsetting his heart as long as you do not believe it. It doesn't matter that you do not deserve it. You certainly don't! But Jesus has promised it!

It doesn't matter that it seems 'too good to be true'; because Jesus has promised it! It doesn't matter if you don't feel as if you had received salvation yet – Jesus has promised it!

All that you have to do is to ask him to give you faith like Abraham's, who was 'fully persuaded' that what God had promised God was able to do. When you do this you will be able to say joyfully, 'This is the promise that he has promised *me*, even eternal life!'

> *Life alone is found in Jesus,*
> *Only there 'tis offered thee,*
> *Offered without price or money,*
> *'Tis the gift of God sent free.*
> *Take salvation!*
> *Take it now and happy be!*

I will love you

'I will love you, O Lord.'
Psalm 18:1

Yes, even if I have never loved you before, I will love you, O Lord now!

I will love you, Lord Jesus, because you first loved me and because you love me now and will love me to the end. Oh forgive me for not loving you! I really should have loved you when you were waiting all the time for me. You waited so patiently while I did not care about you at all! Oh forgive me! And now I will love you always; for

193

you will take my love and fix it on yourself and keep it for yourself.

I will love you, Lord Jesus; I will not listen to Satan, who tries to stop me loving you; I will not ask myself anything about it, in case I should begin to get puzzled about whether I do love you or not. You know that I do want to love you and now, dear Lord Jesus, hear me say that I *will* love you and that I will trust you to make me love you more and more, always more and more.

I have said it, dear Lord Jesus and you have heard me say it. And I am so glad I have said it. I do not want ever to take it back and you will not ever let me take it back. I am to love you always now and you will give me your Holy Spirit to spread your love everywhere in my heart, so that it may be filled with love. Fill me so full of your love that it runs over into everything I do so that I may love everybody, because I love you.

Yes, I will love you, dear Lord Jesus!

My Saviour, I love thee, I know thou art mine!
For thee all the follies of sin I resign;
My gracious Redeemer, my Saviour art thou;
If ever I loved thee, my Saviour, 'tis now!

I love thee, because thou has first loved me,
And purchased my pardon on Calvary's tree;
I love thee for wearing the thorns on thy brow;
If ever I loved thee, my Saviour, 'tis now!

I will love thee in life, I will love thee in death,
And praise thee as long as thou lendest me breath;
And say, when the death-dew lies cold on my brow,
If ever I loved thee, my Saviour, 'tis now.

Certainty

'Has he said, and shall he not do it?'
Numbers 23:19

We have been thinking, night after night, of some of God our Father's promises, and it is very likely that you have been hoping and wishing that these promises would come true for you. But being certain and sure is better and happier than hoping and wishing, is it not? Now, how may you be quite sure that all these 'very great and precious promises' will come true for you? You can be sure simply because God has spoken them! Has he *said*, and shall he not do it? Of course he will! Surely that is enough!

If your father had promised to give you a great treat, would you go about in a dismal way, saying, 'Yes, it would be very nice? I hope that he will do it!' Would he be pleased at that? But if you came again, and reminded him of his promise, and he answered, 'I have said it, and do you suppose I shall not do it?' What a silly child you would be if you still looked dismal, and went on only 'hoping' that he might do it! And what an ungrateful and unbelieving child you would be if you did not say brightly, 'Thank you, thank you so much!' and show him how glad you were about it, and try your very best to be good and please him all day, because he had made you such a kind and sure promise!

When you read the Bible, or hear it read, keep looking out for God's promises. They are scattered all over the Bible, like beautiful bright stars. Then, every time you come to one of them, say to yourself, 'This will come true for me, for he has said, and shall he not do it?'

Before you go to sleep, see if you can remember as many promises as you are years old, and say about each of these promises, 'Has he said, and shall he not do it?'

When you reach the heavenly land you will find, as Joshua said, that 'Not one thing has failed of all the good things which the Lord your God spoke concerning you; all have taken place, and not one thing has failed,' Joshua 23:14.

All that he hath spoken,
He will surely do!
Nothing shall be broken,
Every word is true.

A little boy's journey to find a home of his own

CLASSIC TITLES
Fiction, stories and devotionals

J.C. Ryle Children's Stories (ISBN:1-85792-6390)
Companion Volume to
D.L. Moody Children's Stories (ISBN: 1-85792-6404)

O.F. Walton titles
Christie's Old Organ ISBN: 1-85792-5238
A Peep Behind the Scenes ISBN: 1-85792-5246
Little Faith ISBN: 1-85792-567X
Saved at Sea ISBN: 1-85792-7958

Other Authors
The Basket of Flowers by Christoph Von Schmid
ISBN: 1-85792-5254
Sunshine Country by Kristiny Royovej
ISBN: 1-85792-8555
The Little Woodman by Mary Sherwood
ISBN: 1-85792-8547
Peep of Day, ISBN 1-85792-5858
Line upon Line I, ISBN ISBN: 1-85792-5866
Line Upon Line II: ISBN: 1-85792-5912
Childhood's Years ISBN ISBN: 1-85792-7133
Mary Jones and her Bible ISBN: 1-85792-5688

TRAILBLAZERS

True Missionary stories with a human touch

Bible Classics

Pre-school

The Little Hands Story Bible
by Carine Mackenzie

ISBN: 1-85792-6978;

and Little Hands Story Bible Colouring books

Book 1	ISBN 1-85792-455X
Book 2	ISBN 1-85792-4568
Book 3	ISBN 1-85792-4576
Book 4	ISBN 1-85792-4584

Early Readers

Bible Alive
A series of six books on the person and work of
Jesus Christ by Carine Mackenzie

Jesus the Child	ISBN 1-85792-7494
Jesus the Healer	ISBN 1-85792-7516
Jesus the Miracle Worker	ISBN 1-85792-7524
Jesus the Saviour	ISBN 1-85792-7540
Jesus the Storyteller	ISBN 1-85792-7508
Jesus the Teacher	ISBN 1-85792-7532

Bible Classics

Confident Readers

Bible Wise series
**A series of twelve books on Old and
New Testament characters
by Carine Mackenzie**

Pre-teens

The Bible Explorer
A one volume overview of Genesis to Revelation

by Carine Mackenzie
ISBN 1-85792-5335

***The Big Book of Questions and Answers
about the Christian Faith
by Sinclair Ferguson***

A book for families to discover the key
doctrines of Christianity in a way that
stimulates discussion and helps children wnat
to know more. Parents can sight with relief -
their dreams have come true! WINNER of
Christian children's book of the Year.

ISBN 1-85792-2956

***The Big Book of Questions and Answers
about Jesus
by Sinclair Ferguson***

This book focusses on the person and work of
Jesus Christ from his childhood through his
adult life and crucifixion ... but it doesn't end
there. The story goes on to the resurrection
and Christ's teaching and how it effects us.

ISBN 1-85792-2956

THE

BIG

BOOK

OF

QUESTIONS
& ANSWERS

A FAMILY DEVOTIONAL GUIDE
TO THE CHRISTIAN FAITH

SINCLAIR B. FERGUSON

A new life for Catechisms

If you are serious about your child's spiritual life and education you should review the following material:

My 1st book of questions and answers
by Carine Mackenzie
ISBN 1-85792-570X

Teacher's Manual
by Diana Kleyn
ISBN 1-85792-701X

The Truths of God's word by Diana Kleyn
Student Catechism
1-89277-7231
Teacher's manual
1-89277-7622

My 1st Book of Memory Verses
by Carine Mackenzie
ISBN 1-85792-7834

You will find this is fun and informative
as well as a good foundation
for your families future.

My **1st** Book
of Questions and Answers

'God-centred, Christ-honouring, Character-building.'
Sinclair B Ferguson

Carine MacKenzie

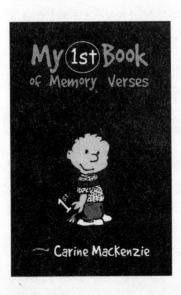

My **1st** Book
of Memory Verses

Carine MacKenzie

Staying faithful – Reaching out!

Christian Focus Publications publishes books for adults and children under its three main imprints: Christian Focus, Mentor and Christian Heritage. Our books reflect that God's word is reliable and Jesus is the way to know him, and live for ever with him.

Our children's publication list includes a Sunday school curriculum that covers pre-school to early teens; puzzle and activity books. We also publish personal and family devotional titles, biographies and inspirational stories that children will love.

If you are looking for quality Bible teaching for children then we have an excellent range of Bible story and age specific theological books.

From pre-school to teenage fiction, we have it covered!

Find us at our web page:
www.christianfocus.com